BITTER SWEET

A Wartime Journal and Heirloom Recipes
from Occupied France

by Kitty Morse

Cover and Food Photography by Owen Morse

LA CARAVANE PUBLISHING
P.O. Box 433 · Vista, California 92084
www.kittymorse.com

LA CARAVANE

Best wishes,
Kitty Morse

Copyright © 2023 by Kitty Morse
Cover and Food Photography by Owen Morse

Library of Congress Cataloging-in-Publication data
Title: Bitter Sweet: A Wartime Journal and Heirloom Recipes
from Occupied France/Kitty Morse

Library of Congress Control Number (LCCN): 2022914894

Identifiers
Subjects: LCSH: Cooking, Memoir, French.
LCGF: Cookbooks, memoirs

Photographs by Owen Morse

Book design by Beau Kimbrel

Book production and printing: Lorna Johnson Print

First edition/La Caravane Publishing (2023)

ISBN 13: 978-0-578-36164-2

LA CARAVANE PUBLISHING
P.O. Box 433 · Vista, California 92084 USA
www.kittymorse.com · darzitoun02@yahoo.com

In memory of Blanche and Prosper

Also by Kitty Morse

Come with Me to the Kasbah: A Cook's Tour of Morocco

The California Farm Cookbook

365 Ways to Cook Vegetarian

Edible Flowers Poster

Edible Flowers: A Kitchen Companion
(First and Second editions)

The Vegetarian Table: North Africa

Cooking at the Kasbah: Recipes from My Moroccan Kitchen

Couscous: Fresh and Flavorful Contemporary Recipes

The Scent of Orange Blossoms: Sephardic Cuisine from Morocco

A Biblical Feast: Ancient Mediterranean Flavors for Today's Table
(First and Second editions)

Mint Tea and Minarets: a Banquet of Moroccan Memories
(and French translation) *Le Riad au Bord de l'Oued*

A Wartime Journal and Heirloom Recipes from Occupied France

I'd never come across another suitcase quite like it. But what was the tattered leather valise doing there, half-hidden behind a crocheted comforter on the top shelf of my late mother's bedroom closet? With its tarnished brass lock already sprung, my next step should have been easy. Yet something held me back. Call it a sixth sense—if there is such a thing—or was it the fear of what I'd find inside?

So it was that the unopened suitcase joined several other antiques in the trunk of my car for the short ride from my mother's home in Oceanside, California, to nearby Vista, where I relegated it to the top shelf in my own bedroom closet. On the third anniversary of my mother's death, I summoned the courage to act.

I set the timeworn piece of luggage on the Moroccan rug at the foot of my bed, knelt down in front of it, and lifted the lid. A label atop a cache of sundry photos and documents took my breath away. Written in my grandfather's hand, it read, *Les Archives Complètes des Familles Lévy-Neymarck.*

Winston Churchill played a small part in the sequence of events that brought the suitcase to California—as the brilliant strategist behind Operation Torch—the Anglo-American amphibious invasion of North Africa in the second week of November in 1942. The military action's success wrested control of Tunisia, Algeria, and Morocco from the Vichy regime *(collaborateur* of the German *Reich),* making the Mediterranean safer for the ships of the Royal Navy and the British Merchant Service and securing the sea as a base for future Allied operations in Southern Europe. Operation Torch also made it possible for the Royal Air Force to dispatch one Clive Cecil

Francis Chandler to Morocco as a technical adviser to newly arrived Free French pilots and aviation mechanics attached to squadrons of British-made fighter planes, called Spitfires.

On official business at the British Consulate, C.C.F. Chandler made the acquaintance of an attractive administrative assistant, a bilingual *Casablancaise* of French nationality. He and Nicole Darmon were married on the 2nd of February 1946 in a civil ceremony at the *Services Municipaux*, Casablanca's city hall. One year later, following his demobilization in London, Clive flew back to Casablanca, arriving just in time to find *me*, Kathaleen Frances Blanche Chandler, cradled in the arms of *madame Bousquet*, my mother's midwife. My father called me "Kitty."

Not long after the birth of my brother, my parents moved to an apartment on the top floor of a landmark Moorish Art Deco building near the center of Casablanca and just around the corner from my maternal grandparents, Armand and Suzanne Darmon, pépé and mémé to me. I became close to both of them, as I did to Algerian-born pépé's extended Sephardic family in Casablanca—his sister, her children and grandchildren.

I also got to know the members of my father's family in England, where my parents had enrolled me in a Catholic boarding school for girls, and where I spent one cold and miserable year. My mother soon realized that Lewiston Manor and I were not well suited and, after the summer holiday, allowed me to rejoin my best friends Joëlle and Florence at the *Lycée de Jeunes Filles* in Casablanca.

My grandmother Suzanne was of Alsatian and Ashkenazi descent. She was wistful and reserved, unlike upbeat and gregarious pépé. I remember the silence that fell over their *salon* on the few instances when mémé's life in France—before she and pépé met—came up in conversation, with uncomfortable looks all around. Even as a child, I learned that this was a subject best avoided. And so my grandmother's past remained a mystery—until I came face-to-face with *Les Archives*, about which maman and mémé never spoke.

Looking up at me from inside *la petite valise* (as I shall now call the suitcase, knowing its French origin) was a photographic portrait of a teenage girl dressed in the traditional Alsatian attire of the late 1800s, complete with an oversized black bow in her hair. On the back was the logo of a studio in Haguenau bearing the handwritten caption "Blanche Neymarck," my great-grandmother and namesake.

Rather than rifle through the valise in a haphazard manner, I decided to follow the more painstaking method of an archeologist and examine the photographs and documents layer by layer.

Blanche's portrait partially hid a pocket-size *Carnet Médical 2ème Semestre 1936*, a medical notebook/calendar printed that year by a pharmaceutical laboratory in Paris and distributed to its prescribing physicians, one of whom was my great-grandfather *docteur Prosper Lévy*.

I assumed it was he who inscribed the title: *Souvenirs de l'Invasion, Mai 1940* inside the front cover and blanketed every square millimeter of the 181 pages that followed with a tight, spider-like script so small as to be barely legible.

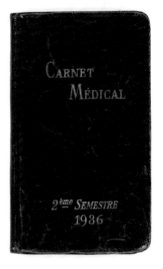

I was about to drop everything to begin the difficult task of reading through Prosper's *Souvenirs* from cover to cover, when I came across the journal's typed, twenty-five-page transcription, a daunting task my mother had undertaken in 1982, with nary a word to me. Her labor of love must have taken months to complete. The posthumous gift allowed me to read through Prosper's journal in a matter of hours instead of days. For this I was grateful, yet disappointed that maman had kept me in the dark.

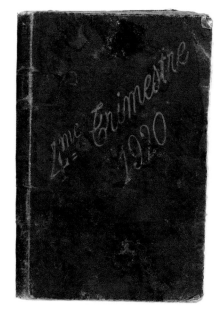

Digging deeper into the valise, I stumbled upon something of inestimable importance to me, as the author of ten cookbooks—another medical notebook, one printed in the *4ème Trimestre 1920*, one Blanche must have pinched from her husband's collection in which to compile her family recipes, written out in a classic cursive longhand.

For housewives like Blanche and her fellow *bourgeoises* living in *Le Département de la Marne*, a region of northeastern France renowned for its cuisine as much as for its wines, being a good wife went hand in hand with being an accomplished hostess, one who maintained *une bonne table*.

Perusing the dishes on the food-stained pages of Blanche's *carnet*, I recognized many that my grandmother Suzanne used to prepare, with no allusion as to a recipe's provenance or to her own culinary training on the *Rue Carnot*. I now know the reason why.

Lacking her first-hand account of life in Châlons-sur-Marne (renamed Châlons-en-Champagne in 1998) I had to imagine mémé's mother, Blanche, standing in front of a cast-iron stove in an ankle-length apron. Strands of her fashionable chignon turned rebellious in the heat of her kitchen, cloaked in a fragrant mélange of a baking *tarte aux pommes* and a *gratin dauphinois* bubbling over with melted Gruyère cheese.

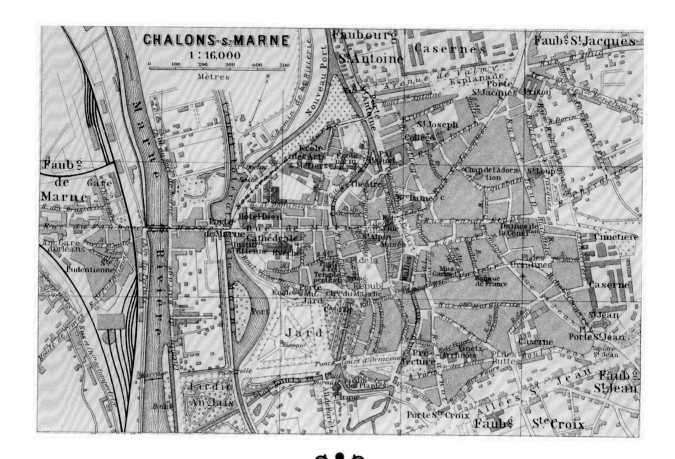

Blanche

Blanche was born in Châlons-sur-Marne on the 28th of June 1871 to Michel and Berthilde Neymarck, the latter a native of Haguenau, Alsace-Lorraine. It was an auspicious time in her country's history. Since adopting the Third Republic, a new system of government, France would experience an extraordinary forty-three-years of peace, as well as political and financial stability. Greater economic freedom, universal suffrage for men, and an expanding economy instilled a sense of optimism within the burgeoning middle class (bourgeoisie). Heightened expectations generated new ideas, propelling France to the forefront in almost every field of human endeavor—from agriculture, architecture, the fine arts, *haute couture, haute cuisine* (like that of Chef Auguste Escoffier), and literature, to medicine, the natural sciences, technology, and transportation, to name a few. To celebrate and to draw international attention to the country's remarkable accomplishments, Paris played host to three *Expositions Universelles* between 1878 and the turn of the 20th century. How far France had come since her defeat in the Franco-Prussian War in 1871, the year my great-grandmother tumbled into the world, at the dawn of *La Belle Epoque* (The Beautiful Age).

What a time to be growing up! Blanche attended the *Pension Raucourt* in Châlons and, after passing her baccalaureate, continued to live with her parents, as was the custom for unmarried young women of means. She'd run daily errands at the *marché couvert* (covered market) to purchase ingredients on her mother's shopping list or pop into her father's butcher shop on the *Rue du Lycée*. Michel Neymarck, a second-generation butcher, was a provisioner to the army of Napoleon III, elements of which were stationed at nearby *Camp Mourmelon-le-Grand*. The name "NEYMARCK" stood out in bold capital letters beneath the carved wooden awning and imposing façade of his establishment. If he and his clerk were busy with other customers, Blanche would slip behind the display case to fill her mother's order for *un*

petit poulet or a few grams of indispensable *lardons*, diced slab bacon. "*A tout à l'heure, papa!*" she'd call out as she glided across the sawdust covered floor to rejoin *Rue du Lycée*.

No doubt Blanche acquired her culinary skill from her mother, absorbing the finer points in the preparation of *vinaigrette* and *purée de pommes de terre*, as I did four generations later alongside her daughter—my grandmother Suzanne. With the choice cuts of meat and the *charcuterie* specialties from Michel's butcher shop, as well as her mother's trove of family recipes and reputation as an accomplished hostess, no one turned down an invitation to dine *chez* Neymarck. After tending to her chores following the evening meal, Blanche was off to her room to get in as much reading as possible before the sandman came calling. This was the routine she followed while awaiting a worthy young suitor to sweep her off her feet. That day was fast approaching.

❧ ● ☙

Prosper

Twenty-five years earlier, on the 3rd of March 1863, my great-grandfather Prosper Lévy was born in the city of Perpignan, not far from the Spanish border. He excelled in his studies and passed his baccalaureate handily, which won him a place in the prestigious School of Medicine at the University of Montpellier, from which he graduated in 1886. *La petite valise* held a photo of a bespectacled young man sporting a goatee à la Sigmund Freud and wearing a white lab coat. Surely, that was Prosper. Had he retained an *accent du sud,* the soft, lilting twang of a native *Perpignanais*, I wondered?

Prosper's maternal uncle, Adolphe Crémieux, briefly held the position of minister of justice in the French *Gouvernement de la Défense Nationale,* an administration perhaps best remembered for instituting the *Décret Crémieux* that granted French citizenship to the Jews of Algeria. Crémieux may have also inspired his nephew to pursue a career in public service.

For that was what newly graduated *docteur Prosper Lévy* did, by becoming a *médecin sous-lieutenant* in the French Army. In 1887, he received orders to the *15ᵉ Régiment de Chasseurs* in the town of Rémiremont, one day by rail from the army *Camp Mourmelon-le-Grand*, with which Michel Neymarck did business, just sixteen miles from the covered *marché central* in Châlons, where Blanche was a regular. Was it here that she and Prosper first met, or had they been formally introduced? We will never know. They were married at the Neymarck residence on the 8th of October 1890.

Blanche was proud of her family heritage and chose to informally adopt the double surname Lévy-Neymarck. In so doing, she would set herself apart from the three other Lévy families in town, none of whom were Prosper's kin. Fellow *Châlonnais,* however, had already resolved the dilemma by linking the Lévy surname with the occupation of each Lévy family's paterfamilias, thereby creating the informal names: *Lévy-Gâteau* for the baker, *Lévy-Bazaar* for the clothier, and *Lévy-Boucher* for the butcher. Henceforth, to the citizens of Châlons, Prosper would be *Lévy-Docteur*. In time, both he and Blanche adopted the convention themselves.

Blanche bore Prosper three daughters: Fannély (who died in infancy), Anny, and the youngest, my grandmother Suzanne. Prosper received regular military promotions and, according to his military record (also preserved in *la petite valise*) was assigned to several posts between 1887 and 1897, including a deployment with the *Chasseurs d'Afrique*, a light cavalry corps in Algeria. Blanche and the girls remained at home. In 1899, two years after Prosper's return to France, he abruptly resigned from the army to show solidarity with an artillery captain of Jewish descent by the name of Alfred Dreyfus, who had been unjustly accused of treason, found guilty, and sentenced to life in prison on Devil's Island, just off the coast of French Guyana in South America. *L'Affaire Dreyfus* was one of the most infamous scandals in French history, one I remember first learning about in history class at the *Lycée de Jeunes Filles* in Casablanca almost sixty years later.

At the time of the Dreyfus affair, Prosper, then thirty-six, entered private practice in Châlons, setting up a *cabinet médical* in his home. He probably made house calls, too, as was the custom, in order to protect a patient's privacy, in some cases, or to lessen the possibility of contagion. Surely, Prosper was aware of the Germ Theory of disease put forward by Louis Pasteur. For all we know, in 1892, one *médecin lieutenant Lévy* was granted a leave of absence from his regiment to hear England's Sir Joseph Lister (the father of antiseptic surgery) deliver the keynote address to honor the renowned French microbiologist at the institute in Paris that bore his name—*l'Institut Pasteur*.

If a neighborhood boy tumbled from a tree and broke his forearm, Châlons's newest physician was available to realign the ends of the fractured radius or ulna and apply a plaster-of-Paris cast. A laborer presenting himself with a nasty gash had his wound cleaned and dressed with surgical gauze moistened with a dilute solution of carbolic acid—a disinfectant in common use before the advent of antibiotics. If sutures were required, thin strands of connective tissue made from sheep intestines were there at the ready, inside a glass jar filled with ethanol. For medications other than disinfectants—oral and topical preparations to provide symptomatic relief from both acute and chronic disorders—Prosper referred his patients to a local compounding pharmacist. He dispensed plenty of dietary advice, too, as well as guidance on the administration of light massage, called *effleurage*, medicated baths, and the application of hot and cold compresses. Obstetrics, a branch of medicine in which he'd had little experience during his army career, became a mainstay of his civilian practice.

When not busy with patients or spending time with family, Prosper followed news of *capitaine Dreyfus*. My great-grandfather must have been encouraged when, in 1898, the Parisian newspaper *l'Aurore* published a full-page open letter penned by writer Emile Zola titled: *J'accuse . . .* , which the Nobel Prize nominee addressed to the President of the French Republic. The letter succeeded in turning public opinion in favor of the imprisoned Dreyfus. Eight years later, he received a full pardon from the French government and reinstatement in the army with the rank of *commandant* (major). Prosper was elated by the news, in part for the sake of the long-suffering French officer but also for his own. I suspect he was a military man at heart who missed the army's esprit de corps. His government's reversal of the miscarriage of justice in the case of Dreyfus allowed Prosper to follow his intuition and return to being a *médecin commandant*, just a few years before the onset of World War I, when his country would be in desperate need of his service.

Meanwhile, his daughter Suzanne, then seventeen, completed her baccalauréate. She'd studied piano during her five years as a *lycéenne* and, according to her teacher, showed an unusual aptitude for the instrument. Such high praise inspired her parents to arrange private lessons for their daughter with concert pianist and composer Lucien Wurmser. So began Suzanne's weekly pilgrimages to Paris for tutorials with the renowned professor.

It wasn't long before international developments on the continent became worrisome, and war clouds loomed over Europe. On the 3rd of August 1914, Germany declared war on France, one day after Prosper assumed the position of medical director of *Hôpital #2* in Châlons, the same day the Ministry of War established the *infirmières bénévoles*, a national corps of volunteer nurses. The Lévy-Neymarck sisters must have been among the first to sign up. For all we know, Anny and Suzanne may have worked alongside their father whenever he was assigned to a hospital in Châlons.

⚜

Hôpital #2 would not be in service long. On the 3rd of September 1914, ahead of the rapidly advancing Fifth German Army, under the command of the Crown Prince of Prussia, the French War Ministry ordered an immediate evacuation of all patients and medical personnel. Most *Châlonnais* followed in their wake, but several thousand chose to hunker down in *crayères,* centuries-old underground galleries carved from thick deposits of sedimentary chalk.

Historian Maurice Pierrat (a contemporary of Prosper's) describes some of the terrifying events in this brief excerpt from his book, *Châlons-sur-Marne pendant l'Occupation allemande, Septembre 1914*:

> It was the start of the somber days when we felt the threat of defeat weighing on our Homeland.... The immense German army is a human flood like an all-powerful wave no dyke could hold back. . . . [Our] town is emptying of its inhabitants. . . . Army Service Corps, hospital staff . . . [townspeople, and retreating French troops] head toward the train station. . . . Infantry, artillery, and cavalry pass by without a break.... [With] the enemy getting closer and closer, there is renewed terror among the three to four thousand [who remain]. . . . Hospitals are emptied of the last wounded men, . . . transported farther away by auto-ambulances. . . . A bomb hits the courtyard of a hospital in the heart of town, shattering all the windows. . . . The last trains leave town, overwhelmed with passengers. . . . Châlons is alone, Châlons is deserted, Châlons is mute, . . . [as] though our homeland has abandoned us. . . . German cavalry [convert] the *Marché Couvert* into stables. . . . Vandals break into apartments, make themselves at home, . . . take what they please . . . and [then make] a mad rush towards . . . our cellars . . . thirsting for our wines, our champagne.

A heroic counterattack by the French Third Army forced the Germans to retreat eight days later. Despite the pillaging and the devastation wrought by aerial and artillery bombardment, *médecin commandant Lévy* and those under his command at *Hôpital #2* began admitting patients again within a matter of days.

Crown Prince Wilhelm's Fifth was not the only German army bearing down on France during this period. On the 4th of August 1914, four others began bullying their way through neutral Belgium and Luxemburg and, after crossing the border into France, were hell-bent on doing the same en route to Paris. For two weeks, their inexorable advance pushed French defenders southward for more than two hundred kilometers, all the way to the southern bank of the Marne River. The *City of Lights* was theirs for the taking.

But all was not lost. The French Fifth Army and the British Expeditionary Force saved the day by executing a brilliant flanking maneuver, with help from Parisian *chauffeurs de taxi*, who ferried three thousand French soldiers from the capital to a widening gap between the German First and Second Armies. The armada of cabs, bristling with the rifles of the infantrymen they carried and piloted by patriotic *chauffeurs,* later became known as *Les Taxis de la Marne.* The First Battle of the Marne, from the 6th to the 12th of September 1914, had been won. The German armies were driven back all the way to the River Aisne, where their troops dug in along the northern bank. By war's end, their network of trenches, as well as those of the French and their allies, would extend from the North Sea all the way to the Swiss Alps. The Germans would never again launch an offensive that held the prospect of turning the tide of war in their favor.

When Prosper's help was no longer needed at *Hôpital #2* in Châlons, he went on to serve as either chief doctor, medical director, or chief of staff at three other army hospitals before returning to Châlons, this time to *Hôpital #19.* His skills were sorely needed. The Battle of Verdun erupted on the 21st of February in 1916, a mere eighty kilometers from his home. The Franco-German duel of heavy artillery raged for ten long months before the French claimed victory—at the cost of 370,000 casualties on their side alone. No doubt, many of the wounded were treated by Prosper himself or in a hospital where *médecin colonel Lévy* was in charge. What dreadful injuries my great-grandfather must have tended to before the carnage came to an end at the 11th hour, of the 11th day, of the 11th month of 1918, when the guns fell silent on the Western Front. Prosper was demobilized seven weeks later, on the 31st of December. For his dedication, he would later receive his country's highest order of merit, the *Légion d'honneur,* conferred upon him by the commanding general at Verdun, *maréchal Philippe Pétain*, who did so on the parade grounds at *Camp Mourmelon-le-Grand*, not far from Châlons. Of the almost nine million Frenchmen who served their country in World

War I, relatively few were so honored, with many of them granted the award posthumously.

The Lévy-Neymarcks, like all *Châlonnais* families, were eager to resume their pre-war lifestyle. Prosper, now a civilian and military *pensionné*, continued to see private patients several days each week. In his free time, he tended to his fruit trees and vegetable garden, played bridge with retired officers in his *cercle militaire*, or read in his study. Meanwhile, Blanche reclaimed her role as a noted hostess, and Suzanne resumed her study of piano with Professor Wurmser, favoring her parents every evening with classical pieces from her expanding repertoire. But fate was about to intervene in the young woman's life.

❧ ● ❧

Armand

In 1921, Armand Darmon, a thirty-year-old vice-consul serving in Marrakesh, French Morocco, was on leave in Paris. While there, he hoped to visit friends at his alma mater, the *Ecole des Langues Orientales,* and touch base with others at the Ministry of World Affairs, where he had taken his foreign service exams eight years before.

My maternal grandfather was a born raconteur, who came from a Sephardic family in Oran, Algeria, a family that traced its roots to Spain at the time of the *Reconquista.* He could read and write classical Greek and Latin and was fluent in French, Spanish, English, Arabic, and Berber even before attending university in Paris. The French government's *corps diplomatique,* recognizing the value of this multilingual graduate of the class of 1918, enlisted Armand into their ranks and posted him to Marrakesh. There, he served under the command of *résident-général Hubert Lyautey,* who was charged with carrying out the French government's *civilizing mission* in establishing the protectorate. Armand's linguistic talent made him the ideal liaison between the autonomous Berber chiefs of the Atlas Mountains, who allied themselves with the French rather than the Sultan of Morocco.

While on leave in Paris, Armand received an invitation from retired *général Justin Dennery*, a comrade-in-arms of Armand's grandfather in the *4ᵉ Régiment de Chasseurs d'Afrique* in Algeria. *Le général* invited Armand to accompany him on a one-day excursion to visit another old friend he'd served with in North Africa, a retired army doctor in Châlons-sur-Marne who had a charming and intelligent daughter still living at home. All this I learned by reading the contents of a large, brown envelope titled, *Histoire de la Famille Darmon*, a typewritten memoir pépé had slipped into *la petite valise*. The discovery was as exciting as it was unexpected, though the contents were somewhat familiar, in as much as our family storyteller had often regaled us with tales of his colorful life among the Berbers.

Armand was delighted by his introduction to the Lévy-Neymarcks, especially to *mademoiselle Suzanne*. All went well enough for her to accept Armand's offer to lunch with him each week at the elegant Hotel Claridge following her tutorial with Professor Wurmser. The young vice-consul had no trouble extending his leave for one month. Three weeks later, Armand made a second trip to Châlons to ask Prosper for his daughter's hand. The two gentlemen wasted no time enlisting the help of a local notary to certify the terms of a dowry. Word traveled fast in a town the size of Châlons, and it wasn't long before friends began to drop by the house on the *Rue Carnot* to offer their congratulations and to admire the stunning diamond ring on Suzanne's finger.

Armand and Suzanne were married on the 17th of October 1922, in a civil ceremony conducted by the town's mayor. The document confirming their union, typed on a sheet of vintage paper bearing the mayoral stamp, had found its way into *la petite valise*, along with a typed copy of *monsieur le maire's* allocution, which he delivered following the official ceremony. Addressing the bride, he intoned:

> Madame, it is now your turn to leave the family hearth to establish your own home. You heard today the article from our civil code that states: a wife must follow her husband wherever he chooses to live. In your case, that journey will take you all the way to Marrakesh. However, I am sure that the company of your husband will heighten the allure of your travels. His mission in the Protectorate of Morocco—to spread French civilization—makes him an indispensable intermediary between the people of that land and the great country that ensures their safety and whose customs, it is hoped, they will one day adopt. So you see, in addition to your domestic responsibilities, I expect you will discover enticing new ways to direct your energies. In conclusion, madame, please allow me, on the threshold of the new horizons opening before you, to express my best wishes for your happiness and prosperity.

Blanche must have spent weeks planning for her daughter's reception. The traditional wedding cake alone, an elaborate tower of cream puffs, called a *croquembouche* or *pièce montée*, would have required hours in the making. My mother prepared the same delicacy for my wedding five decades later.

A French steamship from the *Compagnie de Navigation Paquet* carried the newlyweds from Marseille to Casablanca, where a chauffeur behind the wheel of a gleaming Renault took them on the final leg of their journey to Marrakesh. The palm groves and skyline of the millenary city came into view at a time of day when travelers approaching from the northwest were treated to a visual experience they'd not soon forget. Against the backdrop of snowy summits of the High Atlas Mountains thirty miles to the east, *La Ville Rose*, so named because of the salmon-pink clay that coated her ramparts, turned luminous in the late afternoon sunlight.

Once Armand saw Suzanne comfortably settled into his *riad*, his first order of business was to give her a tour of the city's *médina,* the oldest part of Marrakesh, where hundreds of artisans and peddlers plied their trade within a labyrinthine network of alleyways they shared with donkeys, dromedaries, and other pack animals, amidst an overwhelming aromatic potpourri of exotic spices (like saffron, mace, and galangal), fresh mint, coriander, smoke from charcoal braziers, and a soupçon of dung. The *medina* incorporated the town's *souks*—the markets that Cuban-French author Anaïs Nin described as a "strange mix of din and odiferousness." She neglected to weave in the word *vibrancy*. All three elements were lifeblood for my grandfather, who made the *medina* his home. In time, he became so thoroughly acculturated to the pulse of the Berber city that friends must have teased him about becoming more *Marrakshi* than a high-ranking member of the French government. For Suzanne, however, her new environment was a far cry from Paris and the Hotel Claridge, with a way of life so utterly foreign that she never quite adjusted to its idiosyncrasies, as pépé confided in me many years later.

Suzanne and Armand visited Châlons in the summer after their wedding, as Suzanne was *enceinte* and intent upon having her father deliver her first child, a daughter—Nicole, my mother. Once recovered, Suzanne and her family of three returned to Morocco.

With Anny and Suzanne out of the nest, Prosper and Blanche moved several times within Châlons during the years preceding World War II. In 1939, they relocated to Nancy, the capital of *Le Département de Meurthe-et-Moselle*, in order to be closer to Anny, who lived in the nearby village of Rosières-aux-Salines with her husband, Fernand Cerf, a junior officer in the French army during World War I, and their children, Jacques and Francine.

I've often wondered whether my great-grandparents ever visited Suzanne in Marrakesh, especially during the harsh winters of north-eastern France. There was plenty of room for them in the Darmons' spacious *riad*, and Suzanne could have used their support as she tried to adjust to life in Morocco. My mother, who spent her formative years there, would have been over the moon having her grandparents under the same roof.

Like her father, she developed a strong emotional connection to the city. I remember her telling me wistfully how, "every spring, the Pasha of Marrakesh invited us to his ancestral Kasbah of Telouet in the High Atlas." She looked down for a moment at a photograph of her younger self seated with a young friend on the back of a mule that carried them the last kilometer to the pasha's aerie. "It was magical."

During most of the 1920s and '30s, Suzanne, Nicole, and her younger sister, Martine, like most French citizens in North Africa, led bicontinental lives, returning every year to Châlons, during *les grandes vacances* of June, July, and August. Nicole and Martine cavorted with their cousins along the banks of the Marne and the Meurthe rivers, picked vegetables in their grandfather's garden, and received culinary instruction from their grandmother. The summer of 1938 was especially memorable as it was Nicole's fifteenth birthday. Her aunt and uncle, cousins Jacques and Francine, and her beloved grandparents were there to help her celebrate. Little did she know they would never be together again.

At the very bottom of *la petite valise*, I came across what I most dreaded—a letter dated the 27th of March 1944, one my great-grandmother sent from the French town of Ecrouves (home to a detention camp heavily guarded by Vichy gendarmes) to her dear friend *mme Gâteau* (*mme Lévy-Gâteau*) in Châlons. Blanche writes:

> What can I tell you about our life here? It is such a change that I often ask myself what happened, and if it isn't a nightmare. I don't lack courage, and I can assure [you] that one needs a good amount of it here. Thank goodness I am with my daughter Anny, otherwise I could never have been able to stand this tribulation . . . in addition to these emotions. My husband was not able to withstand [this hardship] and was transported to the hospital in Toul. He has lost his mind, among the living dead, who does not remember me or the children. . . . I wouldn't want them [Suzanne and her daughters in Morocco] to know the hardships we have endured. Prosper, during the night of December 31st, suffered an attack of uremia that brought him close to death. In his delirium, he only called for his children. It was horrible. In his more lucid moments he told me he didn't want to die without seeing them one last time. . . .Will *monsieur Gâteau* have a chance to return to Casablanca? If that is so, we would be infinitely grateful if he would let us know, so we can give him a letter and a photograph for Suzanne.

A rusty paper clip attached Blanche's letter to a copy of an official document titled, *CONVOI N° 70*. It contained a list of names and birthdates belonging to hundreds of French Jews destined for deportation to Auschwitz-Birkenau concentration camp aboard an unheated, windowless cattle car. The word *horrified* does not adequately describe how I felt on finding the names of Blanche, Anny, and Fernand among them. Equally gut-wrenching was the realization that Blanche was deported on the same day she wrote to *madame Gâteau*, the 3rd of March 1944. One month later, 82-year-old *médecin-colonel Prosper Lévy*, recipient of the French *Légion d'honneur*, died alone at a hospital in Toul, a small town not far from Nancy.

Two weeks after that, a sixteen-year-old girl by the name of Simone Jacob, the youngest French woman to survive the Holocaust, who would go on to become president of the European Parliament under her married name, Simone Veil, was a passenger on a similar convoy on the same line. In her memoir, *Une Vie,* she describes the end of her two-and-a-half-day journey in a cattle car: "Upon arrival, we knew that we were descending into a new level of misery and inhumanity."

Young Simone Jacob was transferred to Bergen-Belsen, a concentration camp that British forces liberated in April of 1945. Just one month later, German General Alfred Jodl signed an unconditional surrender agreement at the headquarters of US General Dwight D. Eisenhower. By then, it was too late for Prosper, Blanche, Fernand, and Anny.

Another year passed before *la petite valise* made its way to Casablanca, where my grandfather Armand discovered it on his front doorstep. He recounted the events of that day in his memoir:

> The worst happened in 1946 in the guise of a suitcase wrapped in butcher paper and tied with string, shapeless, half-opened, with no mention of its sender or country of origin. . . . The suitcase . . . contained . . . military records, decorations, some private correspondence, and a notebook where my father-in-law had written down the daily events that took place in Nancy between April and December 1940. This account, written in a lugubrious tone, forecast the oncoming disaster . . . [and was] suddenly interrupted. . . . I immediately understood . . . that it dealt with my lamented in-laws. . . . Our family doctor, a personal friend, begged me to . . . keep the suitcase to myself for a while . . . without showing it to anyone. But, after three months and faced with such a responsibility, I decided I had to act. . . .

The shocking revelation triggered mémé's first attack of asthma, a condition from which she suffered the rest of her life.

✂ ● ✂

Nicole

My mother's large hazel eyes and translucent skin, surrounded by a halo of snow-white hair, concealed a will of iron. She worked as a translator into her late eighties. She prepared her own meals until her early nineties and ate while seated at her glass top table set with engraved silverware and embroidered linens inherited from her mother. She assessed her cooking with the acuity of a professional food critic. "*Elle est bonne ma purée, mais elle manque un peu de sel* [My purée is good, but it lacks a little salt]." A framed petit point tapestry, perhaps a gift from Blanche, decorated her living room wall.

I'd never understood what lay behind the intermittent bouts of depression that plagued my mother throughout her life. How I wished she'd shared *Les Archives Complètes des Familles* Lévy-Neymarck with me, as difficult as that might have been. In 1999 and unbeknownst to me, she reached out to the Holocaust and War Victims Tracing Center of the American Red Cross for help in locating her first cousins, formerly from Rosières, Jacques and Francine Cerf. Apparently, she knew they'd escaped the fate of their parents and grandparents but, after the war, had run afoul of their aunt and uncle in Casablanca. A well-meaning attempt by Suzanne to arrange a marriage between Francine and Armand's protégé, a young *pied-noir* from a good family, led to hurt feelings and a rift between the Darmons and the Cerfs. There'd been no correspondence between them in more than five decades.

Volunteers from the Red Cross hit pay dirt in 1999 and forwarded to my mother an address in the southern French town of Viviers-les-Montagnes. Within minutes, Nicole was drafting a letter to Jacques. A reply wasn't long in coming. Twelve of her cousin's lengthy missives, written in a tiny script reminiscent of my great-grandfather's, lay at the bottom of *la petite valise*. His first letter began:

⚜

> Ma chère Nicole,
>
> As you say in your letter, it is idiotic to turn our backs on one another, since our mothers were sisters. . . . Addressing your question about the family's decision to remain in Meurthe-et-Moselle: you must understand, when France agreed to the armistice of June 1940, everyone believed in *général Pétain*. . . . Few of us in the *zone occupée* would have thought of crossing over to the *zone libre*. Every Jew told himself that he was untouchable because he was a good French citizen [and, in Prosper's case, a highly decorated *médecin colonel*]. Only those who were not good Frenchmen would be in trouble. This is what we all believed. . . .

I also learned from Jacques' correspondence how, months before Vichy gendarmes arrested his parents and grandparents and committed them to the camp in Ecrouves, he himself received an official order to report for a medical examination at a clinic near Nancy. Deemed physically fit, armed guards escorted him and other able-bodied young men to a train bound for Cherbourg. There they would coalesce with similar groups to form a small army of forced laborers assigned to Todt (a Nazi engineering organization) charged with shoring up German fortifications along the English Channel, North Sea, and on the British Channel Islands, then in German hands. During a stopover at *Gare de l'Est* in Paris, Todt supervisors treated Jacques and his confrères to an extravagant buffet lunch, no doubt, in an effort to put meat on the bones of the malnourished conscripts. Jacques wrote of the surreal experience of "dining in the historic train station under an enormous portrait of Adolf" and, one month later, of being transferred to the Channel Island of Alderney, which "made [him] a Jew who worked in England for the Germans." A Todt official on the island assured Jacques and his fellow Jewish laborers that he wished them no harm. "Work hard, and we will provide you with solid barracks and good food." The solidity of Jacques' mattress, cobbled together with sacks of Portland cement, was never in doubt. As to the food, Jacques had no complaints. "We dined on roast pork, from pigs appropriated from occupied territories, which we grilled on spits, while our German guards questioned us as to whether or not we were kosher." Canadian forces liberated Jacques in September 1944. Since trains were not in operation, he headed home on foot, occasionally hitching a ride:

. . . with Americans or *maquisards* [guerilla fighters in the French underground]. I had to walk for two days to circumvent Nancy because of German soldiers still entrenched atop a cinder bank of factory waste near the southern outskirts of the city and arrived in Rosières within hours of my sister, as though we had given each other a rendezvous.

As to Francine, Jacques wrote of how she managed to evade the Vichy gendarmes who arrested Prosper, Blanche, Anny, and Fernand. He tells of kind and courageous neighbors, a wine merchant and his family, the Colins, who sheltered his sister in their home and, whenever menacing Vichy agents were on the prowl, helped her climb inside a large oak cask in their *crayère*. It was *monsieur Colin* himself who, under the cover of darkness, conveyed Francine by bicycle to the mayor's residence in Laneuveville, a town between Rosières and Nancy, where she remained until war's end. At least, this was the story that Francine told Jacques, and he relayed to my mother fifty years later, adding the following post script: "After liberation, many claimed to have played a part in Francine's clandestine life, each one asserting that his or her role was of the greatest importance."

According to Jacques, his sister moved to Switzerland after the war. She rarely communicated with him and cut off all ties with the surviving members of her family in Morocco. She died in 2005.

Following World War II, Jacques became an importer of Italian marble and tile. He married late in life and died a childless widower in 2015, in the village of Viviers-les-Montagnes, not far from Carcassone.

Armand left the French Foreign Service in the late 1920s but elected to remain in the protectorate he helped establish—until 1957—when Morocco regained its independence. The ensuing political unrest forced him and mémé to emigrate to the United States, where they would join their younger daughter Martine, a professor of French literature at the University of Wisconsin. I can imagine pépé holding tight to *la petite valise* as he disembarked the plane at Milwaukee's International Airport. After my parents' divorce, my mother, brother, and I completed the chain migration to Wisconsin. That must have been when pépé relinquished custody of *la petite valise* in favor of my mother but not before inserting a short memoir of his own.

I visited my grandparents at least once every week at my aunt's home, where tea in mémé's airy, antique-filled bedroom was de rigueur. In light of her debilitating respiratory condition, I did most of the talking. Our têtes-à-têtes were in French and covered a variety of topics, from my progress in the Spanish Studies program at the university, to my adjustment to life in America, and anything having to do with food. We often reminisced about Casablanca, an ocean and half a continent away from Wisconsin. I could confide in her about how much I missed my father. Mémé died in her room of a severe asthmatic attack in 1972. Pépé continued presenting lectures at local colleges and attending matches at the nearby Bavarian Soccer Club, until his death in 1975.

My father, Clive Cecil Francis Chandler lived and worked in Morocco for the last fifty years of his life, all the while remaining a proud and patriotic British citizen. For his services to the Crown, Queen Elizabeth II bestowed upon him an MBE (Most Excellent Order of the British Empire) award in 1982. He died in hospital in London in 1994.

My mother died at the age of 94 at my home in Vista, California, in July 2017.

Becoming so intimately acquainted with the contents of *la petite valise* gave rise to the question: what would I do with all the information? The answer became clear. I would publish Prosper's journal along with Blanche's recipes—as a way to memorialize and breathe life back into a family so ruthlessly destroyed and to bear witness to my mother and grandmother's hidden grief.

Granules d'Ephédrine Houdé
Titrage : 1 centigr. — Dose : 2 à 15 par jour.
Asthme, Hypotension permanente

Granules de Boldine Houdé
Titrage : 1 milligr. — Dose : 3 à 6 par jour.
Insuffisances hépatiques, Lithiase biliaire

Je me suis fâché chez notre fournisseur de bois et charbon qui depuis le 1er 7bre nous ... attendre la livraison d'une commande et maintenant il ne ... faudra ... marchand qui voudra bien nous ... et quand? La neige a fait son apparition ... et avec ... que nous en avons maintenant jusqu'au mois de Mai!

30 8bre - 31. Les maisons juives portent maintenant un papillon jaune ... lequel est imprimé dans les deux langues la mention : entreprise juive. Et quand le placard individuel nous signalant individuellement Maroc. Cet après-midi ... la curiosité publique. Et c'est ... quel avenir pour nos enfants si cet état d'esprit persiste chez nos gouvernants. Espérons que c'est un brutal imposé pa...

... autorités occupantes et que la douce France retrouvera son libéralisme d'antan. Mais c'est une bien mauvaise ... qui espérons-le, ne ... pas au moins dans notre pays. D'ailleurs cette ... n'est pas approuvée par la majorité de la population, du moins d'après ce que nous pouvons en juger.

1er 9bre. Journée ... coupée par la ... un couple voisin - Température très ...

2 9bre. Ciel sombre, pluie matinale. Journée ... annonçant bien triste - Toujours sans nouvelles du Maroc. Cet après-midi passé devant le ... Bouchara qui, pendant ... Fermeture ordonnée par les autorités pour ... a changé de raison sociale et ... passé ... mains de ... ou autres; il savait...

Prosper's Journal:
Historical Context

26 August 1939: France mobilizes military reservists.

1 September 1939: Germany invades Poland.

2 September 1939: France calls for general mobilization.

3 September 1939: England and France declare war on Germany.

7 September 1939: French and German troops exchange fire near Saarbrucken.

10 September 1939: British Expeditionary Forces begin to arrive on the Continent for operations in northern France and the Low Countries.

Two weeks later, Prosper writes to his daughter in Casablanca:

> *Chère* Suzanne,
>   On the seventh of this month, your mother and I received news of skirmishes between French and German troops in Saarbrucken. We feared all-out war was close at hand. That same day, Anny took us to Rosières, where she believed aerial bombardment was less likely. We were not alone in predicting that Nancy would be an early target of German planes. However, after the first frost and in light of the calm that reigned overhead, Blanche and I decided to return to the apartment in Nancy.
>   *Je vous embrasse bien fort, Papa.*

More than seven months would pass before Prosper made the first entry in his journal.

Souvenirs de l'Invasion, Mai 1940 à . . .
Recollections of the Invasion, May 1940 to . . .

9 May 1940

French troops have swept into Nancy. The city has come to life. There is a run on boutiques and grocery stores, especially those selling fine wines and aperitifs. Tailors display their finest military uniforms, at prices that scare off veterans of 1914–1918, whose entire monthly earnings could not begin to cover the cost of a *sous-lieutenant*'s tunic. Our officers waste gasoline driving aimlessly around town and fall asleep in the shadow of the Maginot Line.

10 May 1940

0230hrs: The radio announces all-out war. Alas, so cruel. Blanche and I seek refuge in the cellar overnight to the sound of aerial explosions and cannon fire from French antiaircraft defenses. Daybreak restores the calm. In the morning, everyone goes about their business. I turn on the radio. It lights up but remains silent, most likely the result of some explosion in our district. At our landlord's, where the radio has better withstood the bombing, I learn of the German invasion of Holland, Belgium, and Luxemburg. When I come home at around noon, Blanche tells me that Jacques has paid her a visit and so has our dear friend Galissot. Both insisted that we leave Nancy immediately to seek refuge in Rosières [Rosières-aux-Salines, 21km south of Nancy].

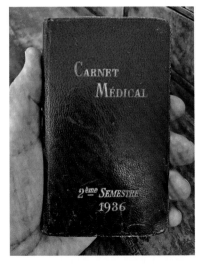

Anny picks us up that afternoon. We settle in at her home with Fernand, Jacques, and Francine to await better days.

In Rosières, we receive news that our troops are in retreat, and our wretched country has been invaded.

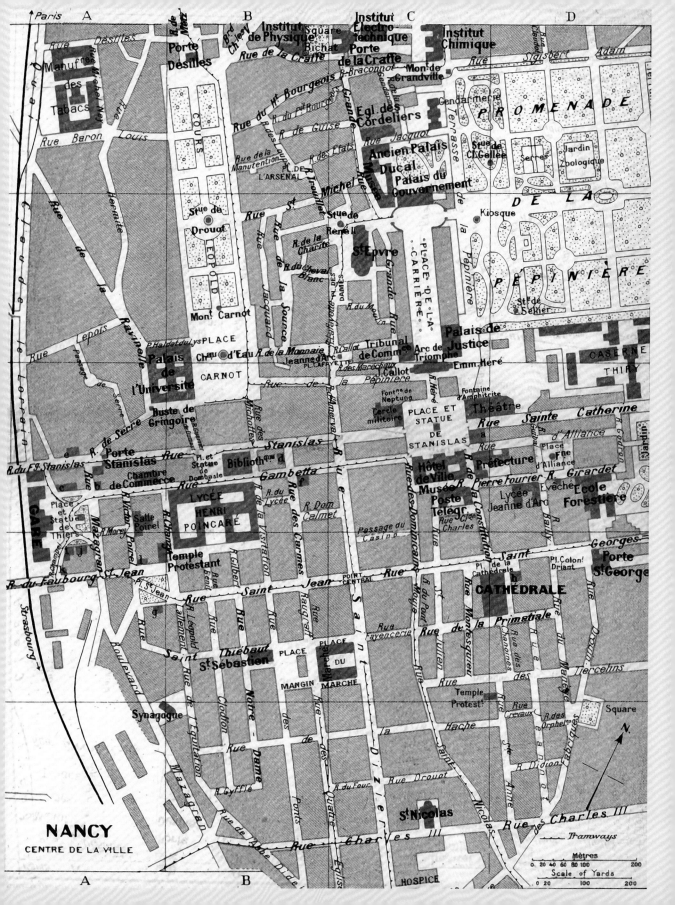

NANCY

CENTRE DE LA VILLE

14 June 1940

Pessimism reigns. Our friends the Davids depart for the south of France. Word spreads that German forces are on the march toward Nancy. All sorts of civilian vehicles, bicyclists, and pedestrians clog every southbound road.

The radio reports that Turkey has declared war on Italy, and that Russia has invaded Prussia or, at least, has amassed troops along the Polish border. Communiqués make no mention of help from our British allies. We are ridden with anxiety. *Le Matin*, the last daily newspaper to reach us, reports the abandonment of Paris. Fernand [a notary] suggests a brief trip to southern France in order to safeguard the last wills and testaments he stores in his office. Anny thinks it best if Jacques goes with him. We stay behind with Anny and Francine. The departure is heartbreaking, but Anny remains stoic. Francine is sad to see her father and brother go but refuses to leave her mother's side.

15 June 1940

Francine's birthday. We have no electricity and thus no radio communiqués, thanks to the director of Rosières' power plant. In his rush to leave town, he somehow managed to disable the facility's generator. And we, his fellow citizens, are deprived of light. This morning, I went to the post office to send a telegram to Casablanca. I doubt that it was sent.

French troops and artillery continue to pass through town. Anny hands out bottles of wine from her cellar to French soldiers running down the road. A cloud of gloom settles over our country, completely isolated from the rest of the world.

The sound of cannon fire gets louder amidst constant air-raid alerts. Italian light bombers strike the Blainville station, where tracks are crowded with trains of refugees, who jump from railway cars to seek shelter in nearby woods.

Sunday, near dawn, we hear violent explosions that rattle the shutters of Anny's bedroom window and shake her bed as an earthquake would. Some speculate that the Germans are blowing up the Maginot Line. Others believe they are targeting the gas depot.

In the evening, we take in an officer of the health services administration, in charge of a detachment from an evacuation hospital in Pont-à-Mousson. He gives us an alarming assessment of the emotional state of our troops and the competence of their military leaders.

We hear voices around dawn, fellow officers telling our guest of their escape from enemy capture and the need to hasten to their assigned post. Anny prepares coffee and bread for the men. Afterward, she maps out their safest route to Neufchâteau. We learn from the new arrivals that Verdun is in enemy hands, that German planes have bombed Vittel, and that all medical personnel stationed there have been evacuated. The men leave at dawn. To the officer in charge I entrust a short note to the family in Casablanca. It was probably never sent. And its courier, most likely, a prisoner of war.

17 June 1940

In the morning, an army lieutenant appears at our door in search of lodging for the officers of his artillery battery. After some discussion, Anny readies two rooms—the dining room, to serve as a mess for seven junior officers, and the study, for their commanding officer, an army major. The men are exhausted after walking all night. They are also charming, distinguished, and discouraged. After their "cook" confesses to his total lack of culinary training, Blanche, Francine, and Anny decide to prepare lunch for the men. Anny serves fresh fruit from her garden, where strawberries are bountiful, and wines from Fernand's cellar. The lieutenant who arranged for the group's accommodations acts as liaison between kitchen and dining room. Despite his insistence that we join them at the table, we refuse, so they may speak more freely among themselves. We do agree to take coffee with them after lunch. They appear most grateful to have gathered, for one day at least, around an elegant table set with Anny's finest linens and silverware.

Rumors circulate that the Germans are about to blow up the bridges on the Meurthe River. Our guests encourage us to leave Anny's after artillery shells land in a field not far from her house. They themselves receive orders to fall back immediately to reconnoiter a nearby hilltop to establish their artillery battery. Blanche, Anny, Francine, and I take leave of the officers to seek refuge at the home of longtime friends, the Grandoeury sisters, where we will be better protected from bombardment in their expansive *crayère* [a cave in sedimentary chalk]. The sisters greet us warmly. We join them for a light dinner and go to bed fully clothed. During the night, we hear a few gunshots and sporadic machine gun bursts.

18 June 1940

Bombardment begins at dawn. In the *crayère*, we join *le curé* from l'Eglise Saint Pierre, a number of neighbors, and a horde of children. The Grandoeury sisters keep close watch to prevent pilferage of their cellar's contents. From time to time, one of the sisters seeks respite in the garden to escape the stale air and chill of the cellar. We, too, take advantage of a lull in the action to warm ourselves in the sun. In the morning, we are free to visit the kitchen for chocolate, bread and butter, tea, and *café-au-lait*.

At 0930hrs, we catch sight of a German reconnaissance patrol entering Rosières, now, officially occupied territory. We no longer require shelter.

Before we take leave of the Grandoeurys' to return to Anny's, the sisters invite us for leftover *civet de lapin*. The splendidly prepared rabbit stew is one of their specialties.

With the battle moving away from us in a westerly direction, we proceed to Anny's via a circuitous route. Rosières itself did not suffer damage from artillery fire. French soldiers, we learn, fought quite robustly east of town in the meadows along the Meurthe River, not far from Anny's.

We encounter an endless procession of German troops, artillery convoys, and vehicles of all kinds. Toward 1700hrs, Anny, who is fluent in German, ventures out to get news. She learns from a German officer of plans to billet his men in the homes of local residents. She also learns of German soldiers shooting several of the town's young men, imprudent teenagers wanting to experience the thrill of battle, exposed themselves to enemy fire. In other words, what happened was not due to German reprisals.

The *curé*, too, puts himself at risk while investigating the circumstances surrounding a pair of blood-soaked fatigues in front of his church. A German patrol suspects him of harboring French soldiers. The priest is held at gunpoint during his interrogation.

It turns out that a French detachment <u>is</u> concealed in Rosières but in a private home. We beg those in hiding to turn themselves in voluntarily, since resistance is futile and endangers us all. The men do as we ask.

20 June 1940

The occupation continues without further incident. I must say the enemy is quite correct in its behavior. Anny serves as interpreter for the whole neighborhood. A German officer with whom she has quite a long conversation, tells her that armistice talks have begun, and that the war is over for us.

Only a few German soldiers are billeted in our part of town, none of them at Anny's.

21 June 1940

It is a very sad day. Compact columns of French prisoners of war trudge past us for hours. In the back seat of a commandeered military Renault, we are sad to recognize the artillery major who spent a night with us at Anny's. We distribute wine and whatever else we can to other prisoners as they pass by.

22 June 1940

The lamentable parade continues the following day. From our window, we notice several men waving at us. We do not recognize them and walk to Anny's fence for a closer look. They turn out to be the administrative clerks to the army major. An obliging guard allows the column to pause for a few moments. For this we thank him. With a rifle slung over his shoulder, he smiles and shrugs as if to imply that no thanks are needed. He looks like an old member of the *Landwehr* [German militia]. He seems to commiserate with us and with the prisoners under his care, who do not appear to abuse the privilege and follow, resignedly, the road of exile. The people of Rosières gather near city hall to hand out bread, wine, and cigarettes as the prisoners go by. All the while, the procession is being filmed, probably destined for neutral countries, to show the Germans' compassionate treatment of French prisoners.

24 June 1940

Although potatoes disappeared from her table more than a week ago, we are able to live off the produce from Anny's garden, especially the peas, carrots, turnips, and lettuce. We'll have green beans in a matter of days. Fruit is abundant, too—freshly picked cherries and strawberries. Despite this cornucopia, I believe that, in the long run, it will be easier for Blanche and me to secure our provisions at home. And so we reluctantly decide to return to Nancy. Anny advises us to inspect our apartment—the only asset Blanche and I may have left after this catastrophe, which many consider to be the end and complete ruin of the bourgeoisie. With a heavy heart, we leave Anny and Francine.

The mayor of Rosières is headed to Nancy on business and offers us two seats in his car. The road is littered with battle-charred ruins and demolished factories in St. Nicolas, La Madeleine, and Laneuveville. An embankment shields two abandoned French tanks devoid of their turrets. Everywhere, bomb craters and all manner of debris.

When we arrive home on *Avenue de La Garenne*, we experience a fright. Our windows are wide open. We see our trusted cleaning lady running toward us. She was there to air out our apartment, which we find in good condition.

In the afternoon, I run to city hall to pick up our ration cards for bread, and I am fortunate to find an obliging employee who tells me that, for the month of June, we are allowed 250kg of charcoal. I go in search of a vendor to arrange a delivery before the first of July.

25 June 1940

While running errands around Nancy, Blanche and I come across German soldiers laden with packages—simply shoppers taking advantage of a favorable exchange rate. They pay with German currency printed with the invasion in mind and only legal in occupied territory.

I noticed a few convoys transporting French prisoners and, clustered inside a school, a large group of French officers of all ranks and categories. They don't appear particularly well fed. *Nancéens* do what they can to help these poor men.

Here, as in Rosières, German soldiers and officers are quite correct and behave well toward us.

26–28 June 1940

When we look out our living room window, neighbors we never thought to set eyes on again pull up on the other side of the street. On the 10th of June, the same day Anny came to our rescue, they packed as much as would fit in the trunk and rear seat of their car and set off for the south of France. Yet, here they are again in Nancy. We do what we can to help them unload. As I suspected, their plans came to naught when Vichy authorities refused to let them pass the line of demarcation. In the evening, we find a basket of fresh strawberries outside our door.

⚜

9 July 1940

Yesterday, I forgot to mention a poster I saw in town. It depicts a German soldier feeding a slice of buttered bread to a child he cradles in his arm. Two little girls smile up at him as they tug on his uniform, as if pleading for their share. The poster's caption reads, "Abandoned populations, place your trust in the German soldier."

Our co-renter on the first floor wonders if she can stay in business, with German housewives cleaning her out of merchandise every time they come to town. The weight of the occupation becomes heavier.

10 July 1940

I meet a friend from my *cercle militaire* who tells me that Radio Toulouse, recognizable because of the broadcaster's southern accent, gave news yesterday of the French parliament's decision to revise the constitution. The broadcaster also reports on a British attack on the French battleship *Richelieu* in the port of Dakar, Sénégal.

Around 1500hrs, I manage to pick up Swiss radio. It gives news from Vichy, where *maréchal Pétain* is still head of government. A secret committee met this morning to determine how to go about revising the constitution. There is also a report on an Anglo-Italian air and sea battle off the southern coast of Calabria. The battle raged for six hours. According to station sources, the British ships withdrew and all the Italian planes returned to base.

11 July 1940

Radio Toulouse reports at 2100hrs that the Vichy government, by a huge majority, conferred executive powers on Pétain and Laval and charged them with formulating a new constitution.

The station also reports on *monsieur Peyrouton*, the Vichy resident-general of Tunisia, who delivered a violent diatribe against England for the loss of the battleship *Richelieu* and the deaths of 1,300 French sailors. He also accused England of backstabbing for its embargo of French ocean liners *Pasteur* and *Ile de France*. This news upset us terribly. Poor France! What does the future hold for her? My pessimistic forecasts, the subject of much reproach from those around me are, alas, surpassed. We are surrounded by enemies on all sides. What will come from all of this? Probably the subservience of France and the whole of Europe. What sad state of affairs awaits us?

Swiss radio reports a terrible Anglo-German aerial battle. The Germans claim the downing of numerous British planes, and the British allege to have done the same to them. Broadcasters don't even bother to mention France anymore. Militarily, we cease to exist.

The station reports that President Roosevelt secured four billion dollars from Congress for national defense.

12 July 1940

I meet with two retired generals, bridge partners at the *cercle militaire*. Both have been of one mind regarding the absolute lack of French leadership and the unconscionable conduct of the British government since their expeditionary force retreated from Dunkirk.

At noon, Swiss radio confirms Pétain's takeover of the French state and the council of French ministers. The British claim the downing of twenty-nine German planes.

13 July 1940

In the afternoon, Blanche and I walk to the post office, where we find a list of *départements* within unoccupied France to which mail may be sent. I immediately write to my cousin in Montpellier, asking her to wire Casablanca to reassure the family about our fate. I will have to get word to our loved ones through my cousin until mail service between Nancy and Morocco is reestablished. Suzanne, Armand, Nicole, and Martine will be happy to receive word from us.

14 July 1940

Sad national holiday! Weather gray and gloomy and, hence, unable to capture French radio this morning.

I went to fetch our ration cards for bread. The walk was depressing, with the city almost dead. I don't have the courage to turn on the radio, as it always functions poorly in bad weather. The day is so long!

In the evening, when skies clear, French radio reports the funereal atmosphere in which Bastille Day ceremonies took place in unoccupied France. *Maréchal Pétain* formally replaces *président Lebrun*.

16 July 1940

At 1030hrs, an endless column of starving, poorly harnessed horses of vulgar lineage pull artillery caissons along *Rue St. Jean* and *Rue St. Georges*. French radio announces that Chancellor Hitler will visit the Western Front to prepare for an invasion of England.

19 July 1940

We learn this evening that postal services to Morocco and Algeria are restored. We will finally be able to get news from the family.

22 July 1940

Anny brings us a letter from my sisters urging us to join them in Perpignan [near the Spanish border].

23 July 1940

We awaken to cold weather and dense fog. We learn that Nancy awaits convoys of refugees from Germany hoping to escape British aerial bombardment.

The barracks in Nancy, once filled with French prisoners, lie vacant, and a municipal employee is making a list of all uninhabited buildings. It appears that finding supplies will become more difficult. Where will that leave Blanche and me with the Franc now at one *pfennig* to the mark?

24 July 1940

The sky is in mourning, as we are here on earth. At 2200hrs, finally French radio is audible again. It reports on the *wonderful* conduct of a group of Vichy deputies who appropriated an oceangoing vessel bound for Casablanca, where they hope to seek refuge. The officials who have brought France to where it is today are among the passengers.

25 July 1940

More rain. When will we get some sun? The first fruits from the south of France make an appearance at the market, including the most beautiful peaches one can imagine! But at what price! Sad. All day long, on railway platforms, thousands of French prisoners are herded into cattle cars, while others wait morosely in the rain for their turn to board.

27 July 1940

Finally, sunshine! Anny receives a letter Jacques posted from the unoccupied zone, where he and Fernand are trying to procure enough gasoline to return to Rosières. Anny believes, as do I, that Jacques should remain in the unoccupied zone to avoid age-related issues. I wrote to Jacques myself saying as much.

28 July 1940

Radio transmission is poor. I caught something about an indictment of former French interior minister George Mandel and something else about England becoming an enemy of France.

We have not read a newspaper since the 13th of June. Our local paper, the *Nancy-Presse,* limits itself to the publication of communiqués from the municipality and from the *Kommandantur* [the headquarters of the German garrison].

29 July 1940

French radio announces the interdiction of train service between the occupied and unoccupied zones. Is it because of the massive assault on England long alluded to in the German press?

From the bridge above the railway station, I see trains transporting imprisoned French officers to Germany.

30 July 1940

Motorized troops passing under our windows on *Rue du Montet* wake us up. French radio reports on articles in the American press that predict an imminent and decisive battle but do not predict the victor. We wait patiently and hope this nightmare will soon be over.

31 July 1940

Good news. The reestablishment of train and road travel between the occupied and unoccupied zones.

1 August 1940

What is in store for us in this, the twelfth month after the declaration of war? It is starting off with beautiful weather. Radio reports tell of new restrictions on baked goods: no more fresh bread, croissants, brioches, and *petits pains*. This does not bother us. Blanche and I eliminated almost all baked goods long ago, happy to have a single slice of bread and butter for breakfast.

Still, the month is starting out badly. A broadcast enlightens us on the *antisémitique* character of a government decision regarding the forfeiture of French nationality by those who left the metropolitan territory [mainland France] between the 10th of May and the 24th of July. Their possessions were seized for the profit of the state.

Another broadcast stresses the existence of numerous Jewish personalities categorized as bad Frenchmen, among them certain members of the Rothschild family, André Meyer, the director of Bank Lazard, and Edouard Jonas, a rich antique dealer and deputy of the Popular Front. They mention only those belonging to the Jewish race. They add a particularly distressing observation, that these men proved themselves Jews before they were French. *Of course, they are not fit to be forgiven!*

Before Léon Blum [a French politician physically assaulted by *antisémitique* thugs and verbally attacked after becoming the first French Jew to serve as President of the Council of Ministers] took office, how right I was to predict that, one day, among our *coreligionnaires*, the modest among us would suffer more than the rich! What is to become of us? It seems our government is moving a little too fast and a little too forcefully. Will we have to abandon our home, the country we love, where we were born, where we happily and gratefully accepted its mores, its customs, its character? When I used to say that we were French by adoption, and that we should remain modestly in our place, wasn't I right? But for many, alas, the success of a Jew, however fleeting, signifies not only the success of one person but that of the Jewish race, and the honor and profit reflect on the whole tribe! Maybe I am being pessimistic at the moment. But shouldn't we consider how repercussion of this publicity may cause malevolent spirits to foment government reprobation, as they have in Germany, where Jews have been relegated to the lowest order, like lepers!

4 August 1940

Our so-called *national radio* is humbly following in the footsteps of its German counterpart. Same style, same stupid jokes, same tendency to lie. We have fallen very low, and our humility is unable to disarm secular hatreds.

What does today hold for us under a dazzling sky? What a contrast with our inner thoughts!

Today, the *Echo de Nancy*, in an article on its front page, reports dispatches from Geneva concerning the appearance of posters in the unoccupied zone that forbid Jews and Blacks access to the occupied zone, even if they have their legal residence there.

On our walk to the *Promenade de la Pépinière* [Nancy's largest park], Blanche and I look with sadness upon the avenues we cross, all devoid of cars and pedestrians. It feels funereal, with Nancy a city in mourning.

5 August 1940

Static created by a neighbor's vacuum cleaner makes radio broadcasts impossible to comprehend. In the evening, French radio is of rare insignificance and weighed down with puerile subjects like England's meteorological psychosis! Why do they overwhelm us with these repetitions and ineptitudes? Everyone we know is sick of it, and, were it not for the hope of hearing a bit of comforting news, one would relegate one's radio to a corner of the attic.

6 August 1940

French radio continues to feed us all kinds of nonsense. In addition, this morning, it brings us unpleasant news—the interdiction, under penalty of sanctions, of correspondence with the unoccupied zone. Believing I had misunderstood, I went to the post office for clarification. A clerk tells me that they have received no such instructions.

On the evening broadcast, French radio, after deploring the shortage of gasoline the day before, now recommends private vehicles make use of *gazogènes* [devices that attach to the trunks of vehicles and generate gas through the partial combustion of wood].

7 August 1940

Trying to get to Rosières. Hiring a driver is not the problem. They all tell us the same thing: "Find me fuel for your errand." Officials in the mayor's office claim they have no gasoline at their disposal.

In the afternoon, we notice that the windows of a friend's vacant ground-floor apartment are wide open. As we walk by, we see several German women inside. Since the apartment's owner is posted in Lyon, it's impossible to warn him and, after all, what would be the use? He will find out soon enough.

The last French radio broadcast of the evening announces Germany's imminent invasion of England.

8 August 1940

Anny's neighbor brings us news from Rosières along with a basket of Mirabelle cherries from our daughter's garden. In the mail, we receive an invitation to pay the charges levied by the government.

9 August 1940

We hear gunshots during the night, possibly related to an altercation between soldiers of the regular army and members of the Hitler Youth that led to several deaths. But these are just rumors.

Evening communiqués from the belligerents announce major naval and aerial engagements on and over the English Channel. The British report the downing of fifty enemy planes. The Germans claim to have inflicted heavy losses on the enemy. We hear similar divergent claims concerning hostilities in the Mediterranean and in Africa.

10 August 1940

We awaken to a tremendous storm following a stifling night. The charged atmospheric conditions will make it difficult to pick up anything on the radio.

A neighbor received a letter from Cherbourg [a city on the English Channel], where life has become intolerable. Every night, residents seek refuge in the nearby countryside for fear of bombardment by British planes. Beaches are unapproachable because of the putrid emanations from corpses washed ashore by the waves. Cherbourg is not alone. All the coastal cities have the same problem.

Morning and midday broadcasts on French radio continue their emphasis on *antisémitisme*.

In the afternoon, a convoy of vehicles pulls up under our window. The private cars, buses, and trucks transport all sorts of people, from the well-educated to farmers, Italian miners, and even a Catholic priest. All await a team of mechanics. What misery!

11 August 1940

A radio broadcast rendered unintelligible due to static was repeated during the day. It stuns us! A German banker is now commissioner at the *Banque de France*. He and his assistant will have their office at the bank's headquarters in Paris. What does this mean? The control of French finances and the end of our government's independence? We have replaced Turkey as Europe's sick patient.

French radio reports on another air and sea battle on the English Channel. The Germans claim the downing of seventy-one English planes while losing only twelve of their own. The British, on the other hand, claim to have shot down fifty-one German planes with the loss of only fifteen. Who are we to believe?

The same broadcast mentions the Italians' military gains in Africa.

12 August 1940

No news from our loved ones in Morocco in almost three months.

At noon, we learn from French radio about the prohibition of forwarding newspapers, even under the guise of wrapping paper, from the occupied to the unoccupied zone. A new interdiction of correspondence with unoccupied France is introduced, about which our local post office knows nothing.

13 August 1940

German air strikes in England continue without interruption.

Our cleaning lady tells us a surprising story: of a young woman traveling on foot between Cherbourg and Epinal [68km south of Nancy] to join her husband. She sleeps under the stars and eats potatoes she digs up along the way. When her valise is stolen, a charitable German officer compensates her for her loss and provides her with a safe conduct pass.

18 August 1940

The letter I mailed to my sister in Perpignan for her 85th birthday is returned. When will we be able to correspond with our families in unoccupied France?

19 August 1940

The great aerial battle over England continues, and the Italians advance in British Somaliland.

20 August 1940

A great event! When we come home at 1100hrs, a neighbor presents us with a gift—six eggs and 375g of butter. Her timing is perfect. As for eggs, we haven't had any in ages. And, what is more, at breakfast, we ran out of butter.

At 1300hrs, bad news on the radio. Under pressure from the Italians, the British are forced to evacuate Somaliland and risk losing control of the southern portion of the Suez Canal, blocking their route to India. Is this the end of the old world—the end of the parliamentary form of government and the freedom that comes with it?

21 August 1940

The Germans extend the closure of the demarcation line between the occupied and unoccupied zones. What are we to make of this?

While crossing the Montet bridge that overlooks the station, Blanche and I notice German troops boarding a train. Other soldiers crowd neighborhood bistros in search of supplies for the trip—white wine, sparkling wine, red Bordeaux, Burgundy, and cognac. Any vintage will do. A few shoppers are already tipsy.

22 August 1940

Our supposed *national radio* is clearly *antisémitique* and Anglophobic. We mistrust the news it brings.

This morning, we receive a letter from our friends, the Barrats, who inform us that Châlons-sur-Marne was absolute Hell for two days. The town was severely damaged and our old house on *Rue Grande Etape* demolished.

The radio announces another wave of *antisémitisme,* in the form of a new law governing the practice of medicine by doctors of foreign origin. When can we expect our expulsion from French territory? My prediction of 1936 has come to pass!

23 August 1940

French radio appeals to citizens to arm themselves with patience while awaiting the restoration of mail service between the occupied and unoccupied zones. The broadcaster conveys the government's empathy for our inability to correspond with our families. Sad consolation!

We meet *madame P*, who is forced to shelter sixty members of the Hitler

Youth in her building. They ransack her renters' apartments and demand the keys to their attics. Since the keys are not in her possession, the thugs break down the doors. Later, *madame P* hears what sounds like crates being nailed shut in the apartment above. The Hitler Youth pilfer three adjoining buildings in this manner.

24 August 1940

An Anglo-German artillery duel employing long-range weapons is taking place across the Straits of Dover. There is no news as to the outcome of continuing aerial engagements over the English Channel.

We learn that a well-known merchant in Nancy who fled with his wife and children before the invasion, returns to find German officers dining at his table, using his wife's best china and silverware, and waited upon by his servants. The Germans suggest he and his family seek lodging at a hotel. Lengthy negotiations ensue before the officers agree to relinquish the dining room and a bedroom. The kitchen is to be communal.

We hear from the same source that a vendor of musical instruments is condemned to six months in prison when the Germans discover a recording in his collection that is disrespectful to *Der Führer*.

25 August 1940

Swallows are gone from the autumn sky. Evening finds us shivering in our apartment. The radio announces a resumption of the aerial combat over England. As usual, no news on the outcome. In a later report broadcast on Swiss radio, based upon a German communiqué, we learn of the downing of 130 British planes, while the German air force losses number only thirteen.

This morning, a German officer, a reservist from across the street, knocks on our door. He speaks excellent French and seems quite correct. He tells us that the unoccupied ground floor apartment of our building appears suitable for his commanding officer and asks that we unlock the door. He promises to return with his superior before they make their decision.

German communiqués announce systematic aerial destruction in England in preparation for a massive and imminent German invasion, bolstered by monstrous cannons positioned along the French coast between Calais and Boulogne-sur-Mer. The cannons have a range of 140km, making them capable of reaching London.

German radio reports that the British have brought into service a new cannon of their own that will launch nets to bring down enemy planes. The broadcaster adds soberly that the weapon has yet to snare a single one.

26 August 1940

The *bureau de tabac* displays unfamiliar newspapers, supposedly from Paris. Headlines provide insight into a publisher's bias. The copy of *Le Matin* I purchased last Saturday astounded me with its contents. It mimics our national radio and repeats the same nonsense.

27 August 1940

The German reservist we spoke to two days ago returns with his commanding officer to inspect the ground floor apartment. We learn that he [the commanding officer] will move in during the day.

This afternoon, upon answering an imperious ring of the doorbell, we find another German officer with a cigarette dangling from his lips. He claims to be looking for office space and enters our apartment without our permission. During his tour, he pauses in front of mementos on my desk. I mention my background. He looks at me without expression. "Too bad this room's so small," he replies. I inform him of the ground floor apartment just reserved for a colonel of the *Kommandantur*. Our visitor says nothing and leaves, cap in hand. From the window, we watch him get into a car and drive off. Strange that he should ring our doorbell, above which is a plaque with my name, and leave the neighborhood without stopping at any other building.

28 August 1940

A workman affixes a plaque on the front door of our building to indicate the headquarters of the *Feldkommandantur #591*. We hope the sign will prevent more unpleasant surprises like the one we experienced yesterday. The occupant of #591 appropriates the garages in the garden. We are, without a doubt, in the occupied zone and now live under the aegis of the swastika.

29 August 1940

Everyone we encounter suffers from the blues because of an announcement on British radio concerning the likely German annexation of the French *départements* of Meurthe-et-Moselle, the Vosges, and parts of the Meuse. In addition, they propose to annex the *départements* of Alsace and Lorraine, which are already incorporated into the German *Reich*. This information, however, is not yet confirmed by official communiqué.

While on my way to renew my ration card for bread, I read an announcement that we will need a ration card for butter. If distributed as regularly as sugar, we won't receive as much as promised. Happy days ahead when we must content ourselves with a dry crust of bread for breakfast.

30 August 1940

I was remiss in stating that since the 27th of August, Blanche and I have done without our *demi-tasse* of coffee after lunch. Who knows when we may resume this ritual? Malt, the coffee substitute now for sale in grocery stores, does not appeal to us.

For several days, we notice long trains consisting of both passenger and cattle cars loaded with expatriates traveling eastward to Alsace.

31 August 1940

Our new neighbor, the German colonel on the ground floor, resets the timer for the stairwell lighting to suit his personal convenience. Nevertheless, we will take advantage of the lights as long as the RAF [British Royal Air Force] doesn't pick a fight with us.

1 September 1940

What does the new month have in store? If only it would bring us the means to correspond with our loved ones. Shouldn't we be provided the same privileges as prisoners of war, who, under certain conditions, are allowed to exchange mail with their families? Our inability to do so is the most painful restriction.

We observe German officers, guards, secretaries, and aides-de-camp leaving a military canteen across from our building. They carry red packages identical to those containing the coffee we used to buy at the grocery store. It turns out the contents come from the warehouse of a prominent grocery store chain. Through requisition or through pilferage, I wonder?

2 September 1940

Delivery of our ration of charcoal is four months behind schedule due to inadequate supply, or so I am told. We face the same dilemma with sugar and butter.

The Hitler Youth leave our neighborhood and board a train, destination unknown.

In the afternoon, Blanche and I bump into a Jewish woman, *madame P*, who tells us in great confidence that she heard from an authoritative source that Nancy is to be annexed by the Germans, who plan to expel Jewish merchants and seize all their goods. She herself has turned over her most precious items to a Catholic friend for safekeeping.

When we part company with *madame P*, Blanche and I are thoroughly depressed by the prospect of fleeing Nancy with only a few pieces of hand luggage and the clothes on our backs. We seek out a bench in *la Pépinière* to recover and discuss the options for safeguarding or valuables.

Thank goodness, Blanche has the good idea to drop in on friends, who brighten our mood by reminding us that whatever *madame P* told us may be lies propagated by subversive agents of the fifth column [a group whose members support the enemy of the country in which they live].

3 September 1940

The first butter distribution in Nancy proceeds in alphabetical order. All goes well according to the happy beneficiaries. We hope this continues when our names are called.

4 September 1940

We find four or five trucks parked along the *Rue St. Dizier*. They are loaded with French rifles and machine guns with their magazines removed. Sad wreckage of our national disaster! Other trucks coming from the French interior overtake us. They are laden with tires bound for Germany.

5 September 1940

Is there no radio station that recalls the events of the 4th of September 1870—the founding of the Third Republic? Are we one, still? *Maréchal P* bears the title *Chef de l'Etat Français*, while he bans the word "*République*" in official acts.

On our afternoon walk, as Blanche and I pass the market, a red poster captures our attention. It informs the citizens of Nancy, in French and German, that a farm boy from the surrounding area was condemned to death and shot that morning. His crime: cutting the phone lines of the occupying army.

6 September 1940

We receive 250g of butter, our ration for ten days. We are now waiting for sugar. Oh, for a *demi-tasse* of coffee and a cigarette after lunch!

What we hear in a French radio report at 1900hrs makes us uneasy. The government, it seems, is reconsidering the Jewish question and certain decrees dating back to Napoleon I and the Portalis reports [Jean Etienne-Marie Portalis, one of the drafters of the French civil code]. But they forget the dead and wounded of 1914–1918 and the loyalty of the truly French Jews that Anatole Leroy-Beaulieu qualified as *déjudaïsés* in an interesting article on *antisémitisme* that appeared decades ago [in 1897] in the *Revue des Deux Mondes*. I remember reading it while stationed in Algeria as a young officer.

7 September 1940

French radio reports on ministerial reorganization in Vichy and the progressive elimination of the last republican elements of the government, in which Laval [the architect of the Vichy government's collaboration with Germany] is becoming more dominant. His first act deals with citizens in *le train de déchus* [the train of fallen], those stripped of their French nationality, including five members of the De Rothschild family, who are considered warmongers. He identifies them as Edouard, Maurice, Robert, Henri, and Philippe, and other well-known Jews like David Weill, two members of the Stern family, and renowned antique dealer Edouard Jonas. What is our government preparing to do? How much influence do the Germans and the Italians have over the spirit of our government? Each day brings its own trouble. We must resign ourselves to biding our time while dreading the worst.

We learn thirdhand of a recent RAF bombardment of Châlons-sur-Marne that caused numerous casualties, especially among the occupying troops. It also resulted in serious damage to the town and put the railway line there out of commission.

8 September 1940

Radio broadcasts focus on the De Rothschild family and the house arrest of Reynauld, Daladier, and *général Gamelin* in a château near Châtel-Guyon. At noon, a commentator reads a new list of those stripped of their French nationality.

The relentlessness of the Anglo-German aerial battle continues. Their respective capitals live under constant alert. What will happen to life in these cities if this situation drags on through the winter?

While running errands, Blanche and I seek refuge from the rain at a *kiosque* that displays the day's headlines. They are enough to fill you with disgust for the press until your dying day. Few newspapers have the *honor* of being distributed in the occupied zone, among them *Le Matin* and *Paris Soir*, as well as one or two new ones which, I am sure, will have but a brief existence.

9 September 1940

We wake to dark clouds and heavy rain. Another *good day* ahead. The Anglo-German aerial battle is as intense as ever but leads to nothing conclusive.

10 September 1940

We receive instructions pertaining to our ration cards for meat. From now on, four days each week, we are allowed 150g of meat (or fat) per person. I find it amusing that babies in their cribs receive the same ration. No exceptions allowed!

We manage to obtain 50g of coffee. What luck!

12 September 1940

The Anglo-German duel continues unabated and is as fierce as ever. The war of destruction goes on. Berlin and London are bombed in turn.

I pick up our ration cards for meat: 150g with the bone or 100g without. We are reduced to the bare minimum.

13 September 1940

I take the train to Rosières. I am happy to spend time with Anny and Francine after weeks of separation. My daughter refuses to turn on her radio, so I will have to wait until my return to Nancy to receive news of the world.

14 September 1940

On the train home, I meet several young pharmacists and auxiliary doctors just released from German captivity. They are hungry for news, but I have none to give. Instead, I tell them a joke I heard from Anny. Question: "What is the new name for *Paris Soir*?" Answer: "*Pourrissoir* [a pile of compost]."

15 September 1940

Restrictions on natural gas force us to rise each morning before dawn in order to make breakfast and heat enough water for our wash-basin. When will our lives return to normal?

French radio reports the Italian attack on British and Free French forces in Egypt.

16 September 1940

Still no sugar. We received only half of our August ration. This morning, however, while running errands, I saw grocers pulling carts loaded with packages labeled "SAY" [after Louis Say, founder of the country's largest sugar distillery]. Who will be the lucky recipients? Not me, because I am unwilling to stand in line for hours to get it.

When I visited Anny in Rosières, she gave me 250g of coffee. A real windfall! We are still awaiting our delivery of charcoal.

This evening, I witness a distressing spectacle, as Brownshirts [members of a violent paramilitary group attached to the Nazi party] prevent cyclists from riding through intersections without stopping, even though the road is clear. Those who fail to obey have their tires deflated by the sneering, note-taking Brownshirts. I can tell that bystanders would like to do something quite different. A local policeman looks on, next to his German counterpart, who exhibits no affability whatsoever.

In their latest communiqué, the British claim to have downed 175 enemy planes against a loss of 40 planes of their own. The Germans admit to only 40 losses while downing 75 planes belonging to the RAF.

The Italians have a triumphant air in their broadcast, predicting, with great confidence, "sensational" events in Egypt.

17 September 1940

Our cleaning lady also works for the colonel from the *Kommandantur*. She shows us his note asking her to purchase fruit from the market and reminding her that "German soldiers are *benefactors*."

18–19 September 1940

We hear that many German families are fleeing the bombed cities in their homeland to seek refuge in occupied France. Quite a few refugees have already reached Nancy, and, from what we understand, substantial numbers of them have found their way to Paris and Dijon.

20 September 1940

Our butter ration is half of what it was in August and our sugar ration cut by two-thirds. Thankfully, we have become less fond of sweets.

The government promises to distribute ration coupons for national brands of coffee, soap, oil, and fats, among other commodities. At this rate, housewives will need a special billfold to hold all the little tickets, made all the more precious because of the trivial quantities involved.

21 September 1940

The storm continues. Rain and wind rage. We finally obtain our September ration of sugar, which is reduced to 500g per person. I am not allowed an old age supplement.

Our thermometer shows 18°C [64°F] with the windows open. Everyone we know thinks twice about lighting a fire, which seems superfluous to us in such mild weather. Yet, we notice smoke coming from the chimney of the house next door that is occupied by German officers. With France bearing the cost, why should they care?

22 September 1940

German radio reports the downing of more than 2,000 British planes in the past six weeks. Yet, the broadcaster fails to report on German losses. This evening, British radio announces the destruction of 1,700 German planes for the same period without accounting for British losses.

23 September 1940

A hand-written notice posted outside the central police station *invites* any of Nancy's Jews, those who have not been officially identified as Jews by the local police, to report to the station with their identity papers on the 23rd of September, at 0800hrs.

I enter the station to learn more. A courteous inspector is unable to find my name on the list he received from Nancy's chief Rabbi. I am not listed, I tell him, because I am not a practicing Jew and, hence, not a member of the Rabbi's community. I also make it clear that I do not mean to deny my heritage.

24 September 1940

Radio reports the bombardment of Dakar [Sénégal] by the British fleet, accompanied by *général Charles de Gaulle* and his Free French Marines. De Gaulle and his British counterpart issue an ultimatum demanding the Vichy governor hand over the colony to Allied forces. I wonder if the British hope to use Dakar as a bargaining chip in future negotiations with Germany, at our expense. Or might they be looking for a maritime base on the Atlantic coast, in light of their loss of the Suez Canal?

More distressing news: the German colonel in our building is leaving and turning over his apartment to three young German secretaries.

25 September 1940

Général de Gaulle's attempt to land Free French Marines on the coast of Senegal is thwarted by Vichy bombardment. De Gaulle calls off the invasion to avoid further bloodshed between the warring French factions. As of this morning, the battle continues.

There is a good deal of activity on the home front as the three German secretaries move into our building.

26 September 1940

We must light a fire in the dining room stove due the cold, rainy weather of the past few days. With our meager supply of fuel, how will we keep warm this winter?

The news is not uplifting. The battle continues in Dakar. In Vichy, the government responds by ordering the aerial and naval bombardment of Gibraltar. At 1300hrs, French radio reports the British retreat from Dakar after suffering serious losses.

We learn from Anny of a Jewish census in Rosières. German inspectors discover that virtually every safety deposit box in Nancy is empty.

27 September 1940

The Dakar affair ends to the detriment of the British.

Over the English Channel, the aerial duel between England and Germany continues.

28 September 1940

Winter hours return in eight days, making our evenings seem interminable.

Swiss radio reports that the British shot down more than 100 enemy planes yesterday. The broadcaster quotes an article from an Italian newspaper concerning the possibility of negotiations between *maréchal Pétain* and the Count of Paris for the restoration of the French monarchy.

30 September 1940

The month ends with true fall weather, gray and cool, leaving us with no pleasant memories and nothing to suggest an amelioration of our fate. We are no longer at war, yet a good part of our country still suffers the horrors of battle. What will remain of our cities on the English Channel and Atlantic that are subjected to continuous bombardment by British planes?

We have had no news of our family in Morocco for five months.

1 October 1940

News of the war is as confusing as ever. We wonder when the merciless destruction will end?

A strong northerly wind and freezing temperatures force us to light our stove. The new charcoal ration of 50kg per month is the only subject of conversation among people we meet. Harsh days lie ahead!

We do get some comforting news—the possible end to our postal isolation. I await confirmation from the post office before I rejoice.

2 October 1940

The post office is again selling government-issued postcards that allow us to correspond with the unoccupied zone.

Paris Soir publishes an ordinance from German authorities calling for a census of the Jews in the occupied zone. It also stipulates that those who took refuge in the unoccupied zone will not be allowed to return to the occupied zone. I trust my registration at the police station on the 23rd of September will satisfy the authorities.

Proof that a piece of good news is always followed by bad: a Jewish merchant tells me that stores and businesses belonging to Jews will need to post notice indicating the heritage of their owners.

4 October 1940

While awaiting delivery of 250kg of charcoal, I learn that the Germans have requisitioned Nancy's entire supply, which their soldiers unload from barges on the canal. Our own charcoal merchant verifies this after encountering a number of German trucks transporting the precious commodity.

6 October 1940

Our friend Galissot manages to return from the unoccupied zone to resume his job at the registry office. He recounts his emotional adventures and peregrinations to cities in both occupied and unoccupied France. He tells of crossing the line of demarcation disguised as a stable boy delivering horses to buyers in the occupied zone. Blanche and I are happy to reminisce about better days when we used to get together to play bridge.

We have a rowdy night ahead of us, judging by the noise on the ground floor. The German secretaries do not respect our sleep.

8 October 1940

We are able to send a postcard to Casablanca. Will it get there? The happiness we feel is diminished upon hearing news of the abrogation of the Crémieux Decree [granting French citizenship to the Jews of Algeria] and the upcoming publication of a statute concerning the Jews in metropolitan France.

Today, Blanche and I celebrate the fiftieth anniversary of our civil wedding ceremony in 1890. What memories it awakens! Many of those who surrounded us that day are now gone. How times have changed! Blanche and I are by ourselves, alas, to recall with sadness, the time when we were starting out in life, when a future filled with happiness awaited us. Must we have lived until this day to witness all our hopes dashed?

9 October 1940

Swiss radio reports on the progressive Japanese infiltration of Indochina that is forcing the French government to move its headquarters from Haiphong to Hue. How far will we be chased? Our French heart bleeds from the humiliations that confront us on all sides.

Out of the blue, we receive a strange letter from Paris. It's from a *madame Coriat*, who turns out to be the mother-in-law of Armand's sister. *Mme C* will soon return to Morocco and urges us to write to her by return mail as soon as possible, so she can carry news of us to Suzanne, Armand, and the girls in Casablanca. *Mme C* hails from Tétouan in Spanish Morocco and holds Spanish citizenship. Because Spain and Germany maintain friendly relations, she may provide the surest way of communicating with our children.

Our friends the Glotz drop by with a green plant decorated with a few ears of wheat, in honor of our golden anniversary. Sad celebration.

12 October 1940

Yesterday, a German-occupied apartment across the street received a truckload of charcoal. As for us, we are still waiting for our allowance of 250kg. And our ration card allows only 50kg for September. We have had to reduce the amount of butter we spread on our breakfast *tartine* while we await our allocation. It <u>is</u> true that our ration of sugar has increased from 1kg per month to 1.5kg. We also receive a 150g packet of tea from our niece, Cécile Blum, in Paris.

13–15 October, 1940

Nights are quite lively on the ground floor, with loud music, dancing, and drunken behavior. The young ladies entertain visitors during the day as well. This morning, when I came home around 1100hrs, I saw, through the open doorway to their apartment, a German *feldgrau* [field grey] uniform relaxing in an armchair of the young women's salon. It won't be long before they post a big, bold sign on the front of our building. Could the secretaries' apartment be a variation of BMC [*bordel militaire de campagne*—a brothel that provides services to soldiers]?

16 October 1940

Over the course of two days, our cleaning lady finds seventeen empty bottles of champagne, ten bottles of red wine, and fifteen bottles of beer in the young women's apartment.

17 October 1940

Unbelievable rumors circulate in Nancy these days. I'd be taken for an idiot if I took them into account. People begin to whisper when conflicting accounts are broadcast in the news.

18 October 1940

French radio reports on a law to resolve the status of French Jews. It will close numerous occupations to Israelites, even those established in France for many years and to those born of fathers who shed their blood for their country. It's of no use talking about this new law, which is the height of iniquity and deprives us of all our civil and political rights and forces many to resign. What I feared is now a fait accompli. We are turning into French citizens of the lowest order, since our children will no longer be able to serve as officers or professors. How could we have imagined such a thing? This intensifying cruelty and injustice, using erroneous arguments, seeks to attribute our integration into the French nation as the primordial reason for the catastrophe that has befallen our poor country. Let us weep silently while we await the hour of resurrection that my old age, in all likelihood, will not allow me to witness. We hear rumors from various sources that, in Vichy, the Germans reauthorized the use of the French language, which had been banned soon after the occupation began. Once again, we will see French signs above

French stores. We hear rumors that Goering and Rudolph Hess are victims of the British bombing at Le Havre. For several days now, we feel something brewing that is being carefully kept from us and rekindles some hope. We need it!

19 October 1940

We don't believe anything we hear. We wonder, at times, if those around us are crazy, or if <u>we</u> are the ones who have lost our minds. We don't dare repeat anything whispered to us for fear of being taken for simpletons. As for Blanche and me, we wait, as the Arabs do, for Allah's protection.

I have to stand in line in an open courtyard to exchange ration cards. Fortunately, it isn't raining. The restrictions we face are onerous: 375g of meat and 20g of cheese per person per week. Stores in Nancy no longer carry dried beans of any kind!

20 October 1940

All the lies that circulate in Nancy create fleeting illusions, followed by a collapse of all hope. Those around me are astonished and frequently upset by my skeptical attitude toward sensational stories like the one about the American flag that flies in Metz, the status of retired French Jews, and the magnanimity of our occupiers when it comes to the resupply of our provisions.

21 October 1940

We receive a postcard from Jacques. He and his father are finally on their way home from the unoccupied zone. I will be happy when poor Anny and Francine's isolation is at an end.

22 October 1940

Yellow posters, each bearing a Star of David, make their appearance in windows of Jewish establishments. They are bound to discourage German shoppers.

23 October 1940

We hear passionate commentaries on the radio regarding talks between Pierre Laval [vice-president of the Vichy regime's Council of Ministers] and Hitler. There is an outbreak of lies regarding German conditions for peace. Some people concoct them with great satisfaction while awaiting official reports.

25 October 1940

French radio reports on a Pétain-Hitler meeting. Naturally, without providing details. We will wait and hope. When will this nightmare end?

26 October 1940

Anny surprises us for lunch and stays until 1830hrs. In the evening, the radio broadcasts a government communiqué regarding the Pétain-Hitler meeting and, again, provides no details.

27 October 1940

Swiss radio announces a tentative agreement between Pétain and Hitler, and French radio speaks of possible collaboration between France and the Axis powers [Germany, Italy, and Japan].

28–29 October 1940

The first snowfall is a sad portent for the coming winter!

We learn from a radio report that it is the Greek nation's turn to join in the *dance* and get acquainted with the *sweetness* [of the Italian invasion of Greece on the 28th of October 1940].

30–31 October 1940

Jewish businesses now display *papillons jaunes* [yellow butterflies—stars-of-David] with the words "Jewish enterprise" in French and German. When will we have to wear individual badges subjecting us to public scrutiny? This is civilization? What lies ahead for our children if this state of mind persists among those who govern us? Let's hope it is just a diktat by the occupying authorities, and that our sweet France will return to its former liberalism, and that this bad seed will not take root in our country. The majority of the population does not approve of this measure, at least, in my opinion.

2 November 1940

The day is shaping up as a sad one. Still no news from Morocco. This afternoon, I walked past BOUCHARA'S [a Jewish-owned home furnishings store] that had been closed for illicit price gouging. The store, renamed by its new, Christian owner, has reopened. A local policeman stands guard at the head of a long line of women, both French and German, who hope to enter. Inside, among the privileged few, we see nothing but German officers. Other German officers approach a side door, and a second policeman lets them enter. The furious women in line rain invectives on the poor man. Wonders of the occupation! Too bad radio broadcasters are not here to witness the way in which we obtain goods from the occupying authorities.

3–4 November 1940

The rainstorm and strong winds that awakened us this morning will surely curtail the aerial warfare over the English Channel. Fortunately, the barometer is rising, and we can cut back on our use of wood and charcoal.

The home furnishings store looks more like a guard house. Through the windows, we see only military uniforms.

5 November 1940

Finally, a postcard from Casablanca! What happiness to see our daughter's handwriting again after being deprived of it for close to five months. The postcard does not allow detailed correspondence, but it is better than nothing.

This afternoon, we meet several people who give us news of Alsace. Now that the harvest is over, it seems the occupiers are emptying the villages. The Germans propose to transport Alsatians to Poland, where they will receive property of equal value to what they are forced to abandon. If they refuse, their property in Alsace will be expropriated, they will be given 10,000 Francs per family, and relocated in unoccupied France. Terror reigns over the entire region, prompting some grief-stricken inhabitants to set fire to their farms. Others lie on the ground and refuse to leave. For many, it is complete ruin.

For the second time in six weeks, the central police station posts a notice *inviting* Israelites, with their identity papers, to register with the authorities. What does this new *invitation* portend? Is it a harbinger of future expulsion? We return home sick at heart. After the joy we got from Suzanne's letter, is this "cold shower" an omen of an unhappy future? When will we find peace?

6–7 November 1940

Every *Nancéen* speaks of the situation in Alsace-Lorraine, with each one adding a new, more horrifying detail to the expulsions.

8 November 1940

There must have been a fight among the *secretaries* on the ground floor. This, according to our cleaning lady, who found shards of glass inside their piano. Happy life.

A state of siege exists in Strasbourg. The cathedral is decommissioned and transformed into a game room for German troops.

9 November 1940

Blanche and I register at the central police station again, where an officer adds the words "*Juive*" and "*Juif,*" respectively, on our identity papers, in red letters two centimeters high.

11–13 November 1940

Violent wind and rain force us to light a fire. We are filled with anguish to see our small provision of wood further reduced. Yet, all around us, clouds of smoke rise from the chimneys in German-occupied buildings. French prisoners deliver charcoal to the *darlings* on the ground floor.

Since the Alsatians want nothing to do with resettlement in Poland, their forced migration to unoccupied France goes forward. They are allowed 50kg of luggage and given 2,000 Francs to cover expenses, a portion of which they will have to relinquish at the line of demarcation. This, according to *madame J.*

15 November 1940

The first broadcast on French radio at 0900hrs remains mute on the subject of Alsace. Since trains of immigrants have already reached unoccupied France, the world will learn everything soon enough. In the evening, Swiss radio reports that the Germans do not deny their deportation of Alsatians, which they justify with a muddled comparison to the relocation of Germans inhabiting the Tyrolian region of Italy.

16 November 1940

Swiss radio reports that the refugees from Alsace will be put to work cultivating the fields of abandoned farms in southwestern France. The reason for their deportation becomes clear!

17–18 November 1940

In his sermon, the priest of our parish in Nancy deplores the miseries of the "transplanted ones" from Lorraine, whom he describes as "veritable human cattle."

22–23 November 1940

A large, blood-red poster appears in town near the *Hotel de Ville* [city hall]. Its caption: "England, Enemy of Europe" hints at its origin. I don't think it is producing the intended effect. *Nancéens* read it in silence and shrug their shoulders. Contrary to French custom, it omits the name of the printer. The message harkens back to the German war cry of 1914–1918, "*Gott strafe England*" [May God Punish England].

25 November 1940

A new poster replaces the red one, now shredded. On a white background in bold red letters, it reads, "Dakar and Mers-el-Kebir—Frenchmen remember!" The *bleu, blanc, rouge* [blue, white, and red] colors of the French flag frame the poster. We lend it no more credence than the original, and it is defaced just as quickly.

26–30 November 1940

Yet another poster appears, this one depicting England as a squid wrapping its tentacles around Europe and Africa.

Blanche and I encounter *monsieur F*, his devastated visage indicative of the epilogue of his son's misadventure. He recounts the young man's arrest, but as we are in the street, he does not dare go into detail. Suspicion reigns, and we are loath to converse with someone we are not sure of.

French radio reports heavy damage and thousands of victims after bombings in Berlin and in the Ruhr Valley.

It seems the German bourgeoisie is worried about the development of communist tendencies within national socialism.

6 December 1940

Last night, we were kept awake until 0300hrs by German officers engaging in dissolute orgies of cries, shouts, singing, and tap dancing with the *secretaries* on the ground floor. Patrons at the neighborhood grocery speak of how the scandalous behavior spilled out onto *Rue du Montet*.

7 December 1940

Important troop movements at the train station. Are they off to shore up the Italians, who continue to sustain heavy losses?

8–10 December 1940

The Germans ordered the chancellor of the *Université de Lorraine* to deny admission to Jewish applicants.

Toward noon, our German neighbors gather around the radio to listen to a speech by their *Führer*. Spirits don't seem very high downstairs.

11–12 December 1940

From the summary published in the local newspaper, the *Führer*'s speech covered the usual topics—the need for more breathing room for Germany and the collapse of democracies. He is disappointed by Italian losses to Greek forces in Albania and to British forces in Egypt.

We met *monsieur F*, whose son is still in solitary confinement.

13–14 December 1940

Cold weather returns. We were promised three cords of wood but received nothing. Obtaining meat and cheese is becoming more and more difficult. We will soon have to tighten our belts and resign ourselves to our sad fate, while ardently hoping for a miracle.

18 December 1940

Air raid alert around 2100hrs and cannon fire from German antiaircraft guns. We do not seek shelter in light of the bitterly cold weather.

20 December 1940

The cold is so extreme it frightens us.

21–22 December 1940

The weather is so frigid, our thermometer does not move.

News from unoccupied France reaches us with less and less frequency. We wonder if the weekly postcards I send to Casablanca are getting through.

23–24 December 1940

Always the frost. There is no way to obtain our meager ration of 50kg of charcoal for December. Yet trucks unload cords of wood in front of buildings occupied by Germans.

A delightful incident interrupted a matinee at the municipal theater. A young woman received a fine of two-hundred French Francs for shoving, with premeditation, a German officer.

Ran across *monsieur F.* His son will meet with his lawyer on the 2nd of January in preparation for a trial at the end of that month. It seems that he contracted a beneficial mange [a parasitic skin disease] that interrupts the monotony of his incarceration.

25–28 December 1940

The intense cold makes life difficult. Those few who have charcoal complain about its poor quality. As for us, we will have to content ourselves with green wood.

British planes bomb the nearby town of Lunéville.

We've had no meat in two days, but somehow, our butcher finds a way to send us two small lamb chops. We are also able to purchase half a rabbit and a small roasting chicken from our butter vendor. This should help feed us for five or six days.

An eleven-year-old boy running in the street was fined and condemned to one day in jail for bumping into a German officer. With much difficulty, the boy's mother is granted permission to take her son's place.

29 December 1940

A charitable soul brings us three slices of ham.

30–31 December 1940

   The barometer is sinking. Gray weather. The year is ending on a sad note. Blanche and I are preoccupied with finding enough fuel to feed both our stomachs and our stove. There are lines in front of every grocery store in Nancy. Fuel supplies are exhausted. At the same time, the Germans drive around with trucks filled with charcoal.

   Surprise this afternoon: the year ends on an optimistic note. Our vendor delivers two sacks of wood. But, at what price! And our butcher, fearing we would die of hunger, sends us a roast beef, unaware of the whole chicken in our pantry. What else can happen between the end of 1940 and the dawn of a new year?

   New Year's Eve 1940 marked the last time Prosper put pen to paper in his *carnet médical*. This didn't surprise me. I'd noticed how his journal entries had become more sporadic with the onset of cold weather. My great-grandfather was 78 years old, likely experiencing early symptoms of dementia, and trying to survive in a city where living conditions had become increasingly harsh. Something had to give, and that was the *Souvenirs de l'Invasion*. Prosper died in the town of Toul three years later.

Blanche's Recipes

I was so overwhelmed by the bonanza of my great-grandmother's recipes that my initial reading of her cookbook was less than comprehensive. I'd failed to realize how heavily weighted it was with desserts, which inspired me to put together the following census:

Tally of All Recipes • 146

Chocolate Cakes • 16

Other Cakes • 44

Cookies • 33

Crêpes • 2

Other Desserts • 31

Breads and Crackers • 14

Savory Dishes • 6

The tally was hardly what I'd expected from a woman whose father (my great-great-grandfather) supplied meat and poultry to the armies of Napoleon III. I wondered whether Blanche devoted another notebook to *soupes*, *salades*, *accompagnements,* and *entrées.* If so, was it overlooked in an otherwise empty drawer in the Nancy apartment—inadvertently orphaned by the kind soul who took it upon himself to pack and deliver the Lévy-Neymarck archives to Casablanca?

All this to say that the recipes contained in Blanche's notebooks were

not indicative of the meals she prepared for her daughters and later, for her granddaughters, during the many *grandes vacances* they spent in France. Thus, I took the liberty of including a number of savory dishes well-known to the bourgeoises of *Le Grand Est*, as well as to Suzanne and Nicole, who'd spent many hours serving "apprenticeships" in the Lévy-Neymarck kitchen and, years later, prepared the same dishes for me.

The recipes from my great-grandmother's notebook provided me with insight into Suzanne and Nicole's penchant for desserts, especially those containing chocolate! Their predilection lives on. At home in California, *Bûche de Noël*, taught to me by my grandmother Suzanne, graces our table, not only as a holiday dessert, but also as a *Bûche d'Anniversaire* and, more recently, as a *Bûche de Triomphe* to celebrate the publication of *Bitter Sweet*.

I'm sure that my great-grandmother's handwritten recipes were meant for her private use and not for a memoir-with-food published in America and printed in China close to 80 years after her death. If she'd had a crystal ball, she would have provided American equivalents for her metric weights and measures and greatly expanded upon her methods of preparation. I have corrected both oversights while testing the recipes in my own kitchen.

Note: My great-grandparents lived secular lives. They did not keep a Kosher kitchen nor did they follow the dietary guidelines set forth in Leviticus and Deuteronomy.

Beignets de Carnaval
Vendredi 3 Décembre. — S. François X.

1845. — Weber découvre l'action d'arrêt du pneumo-gastrique.

Pour 2 plats de beignets mettez 2 cuillères sucre en poudre, le faire fondre avec un peu d'eau - ajouter 96 grains de sel, un peu de rhum - Mettre ensuite 3 œufs entiers qu'on délaye bien avec le sucre et ajouter de la farine pour avoir une pâte bien ferme - Couper en morceaux gros comme une noix pétrisser de nouveau étendez en galettes très minces chaque noix de pâte et rayez avec la roulette en ayant soin que les raies s'arrêtent à 1 cm des bords de la galette. Faire cuire les galettes dans de la friture bien chaude. Saupoudrez de sucre à volonté

Clafoutis
Mercredi 29 Décembre. — S. Thomas de C.

1669. — Mort à Londres de Sydenham (Thomas), à l'âge de 65 ans; il était né en 1604 à Windsor-Eagle (comté de Dorset); il donna la manière d'administrer le quinquina dans les fièvres intermittentes et fit paraître, en 1669, la formule du laudanum qui porte son nom.

Verser 240g farine en ménageant un trou au milieu - Y mettre 3 jaunes d'œufs, un peu de sel, tourner en ajoutant de l'eau pr que la pâte ait la consistance d'une pâte à beignets - Ajoutez 2 cuillers d'eau de vie, les blancs d'œufs en neige, le sucre, et 750 de cerises noires dénoyautées et sans queues. Verser le tout dans un plat émaillé beurré et disposez dessus de petits morceaux de beurre. Cuire à four modéré 1/2 heure. Se sert chaud ou froid - + 50g sucre

Chapter One

Soups, Salads, and Savory Pastries

Velouté aux Champignons
Mushroom Soup

Salade d'Endives du Nouvel An
New Year's Eve Endive Salad

Poireaux Vinaigrette
Leeks Vinaigrette

Salade de Chou à l'Alsacienne
Alsatian Cabbage Salad

Tartelettes aux Lardons et aux Poireaux
Lardons and Leek Tartlets

Tarte à l'Oignon
Onion Tart

Flammekueche/Tarte flambée
Alsatian Flatbread

Crêpes aux Champignons et au Jambon
Mushroom and Ham Crêpes

Oeufs Brouillés
Scrambled Eggs

Strudel Rouge et Vert
Red and Green Cabbage Strudel

Choux aux Crevettes
Curried Shrimp Puffs

Potage de Pommes de Terre à l'Oseille
Leek and Potato Soup with Sorrel

⚜

Velouté aux Champignons
Mushroom Soup

SERVES 4

4 ounces fresh morel mushrooms
12 ounces cremini mushrooms,
 wiped clean
4 tablespoons unsalted butter,
 divided use
1 garlic clove, minced
½ medium onion, diced
4 cups chicken broth
1 chicken bouillon cube

1 medium potato,
 peeled and diced
1 teaspoon salt
⅛ teaspoon freshly ground
 black pepper
¼ cup sherry, for serving
Crème fraîche, for serving
Fresh thyme leaves, for garnish

Rinse the morels under running water and drain. Dry with a paper towel. Thinly slice the morels and the cremini mushrooms. In a small skillet over medium heat, melt 2 tablespoons of the butter and cook the mushrooms until golden. Remove from the heat and set aside 8 slices of the cremini mushrooms for garnish.

In a large saucepan over medium heat, melt the remaining butter. Add the garlic, onion, chicken broth, bouillon cube, and diced potato. Cook until the potato is soft, 12 to 14 minutes. Remove from the heat and let cool.

In a blender or food processor, in increments, purée the potato mixture with the morels and cremini mushrooms until smooth. Season with salt and pepper. Return the soup to the saucepan and heat through. To serve, ladle into individual bowls and stir 2 teaspoons of sherry into each one. Garnish with the reserved cremini slices, a dollop of crème fraîche, and the thyme leaves. Serve hot.

Sidebar: Fresh or dried morels add a subtle earthiness to this *velouté*, from the French word *velours* (velvet). Foraging for wild fungi remains a popular pastime in northeastern France, especially in the forests near Haguenau, where the damp, alluvial soil provides an ideal environment for morels.

Salade d'Endives du Nouvel An
New Year's Eve Endive Salad

Serves 4

4 Belgian endives
2 teaspoons Dijon mustard
2 tablespoons white wine vinegar
3 tablespoons walnut oil
¼ teaspoon salt
⅛ teaspoon freshly ground
    black pepper

1 teaspoon dried tarragon leaves,
    crushed
4 ounces lardons (see Note)
¼ cup walnut pieces, toasted
¼ cup crumbled Roquefort cheese

Clean the endives with a damp cloth. Do **not** soak them in water. Trim and discard ¼ inch from the root end. Cut 1½ inches from the leafy tips and set aside. Cut the rest of the endives into rounds ½ inch thick. Set aside.

Whisk the mustard and vinegar until smooth. Continue to whisk while adding walnut oil, in a stream, until the mixture is emulsified. Stir in salt, pepper, and tarragon. Set the dressing aside.

In a small skillet over medium heat, cook the lardons until crisp, 5 to 6 minutes. Remove from the heat and drain on a paper towel.

Separate the endive rounds into rings and arrange in the center of a serving platter. Surround them with the leafy endive tips. Drizzle with dressing and sprinkle with toasted walnuts, crumbled Roquefort, and lardons.

Note: Lardons (short, ¼ to ⅓-inch-thick pieces of slab bacon) are used extensively in French cooking and are available in butcher shops, specialty markets, and online. Or make them at home from slab bacon, rind removed. Substitute diced pancetta if you prefer.

Poireaux Vinaigrette
Leeks Vinaigrette

SERVES 4

8 slender French leeks (see Note),
    trimmed of roots
1 teaspoon Dijon mustard
1 tablespoon white wine vinegar
½ teaspoon salt
¼ teaspoon freshly ground
    black pepper

2 tablespoons vegetable oil
1 tablespoon minced parsley
One hard-boiled egg,
    finely chopped

Thoroughly rinse the leeks under running water to remove all traces of soil. Put them in a medium saucepan, cover with water, and bring to a low boil. Cook until leeks are tender, 10 to 15 minutes, and set aside to drain.

In a bowl, whisk together the mustard, vinegar, salt, and pepper. While continuing to whisk, add the vegetable oil until the vinaigrette is emulsified.

Transfer the leeks to a relish dish. Drizzle with vinaigrette and garnish with parsley and chopped hard-boiled egg. Serve at room temperature.

Note: Slender leeks, less than ½ inch in diameter, are more tender and have a milder flavor than those harvested later in the season. Look for these delicate *poireaux* in the spring and fall at farmer's markets and specialty markets.

Salade de Chou à l'Alsacienne
Alsatian Cabbage Salad

SERVES 4

2 teaspoons Dijon mustard

1 teaspoon salt

½ teaspoon freshly ground
    black pepper

2 teaspoons granulated sugar

1 garlic clove, minced

2 tablespoons white wine vinegar

1 tablespoon water

⅔ cup vegetable oil

1 small red cabbage, trimmed

1 small green cabbage, trimmed

8 baby potatoes, boiled and
    cut in half

4 radishes, thinly sliced

3 hard-boiled eggs, peeled
    and cut into wedges

2 ounces Gouda cheese,
    cut into matchsticks

2 ounces Gruyère cheese, cubed

4 slices cervelat or any other
    cured cold cuts

8 sprigs parsley, minced

Edible flowers, for garnish

In a medium bowl, whisk together the mustard, salt, pepper, sugar, garlic, vinegar, and water. While continuing to whisk, add the vegetable oil until the vinaigrette is emulsified. Set aside.

Carefully separate 8 whole leaves from the red cabbage and set aside. Thinly slice one quarter of the remaining red cabbage and save the rest for another use. Thinly slice half of the green cabbage and save the rest for another use. Soak the sliced red and green cabbage in a large bowl of lightly salted water for 30 minutes. Drain and set aside.

To assemble the salad, arrange the whole red cabbage leaves on the perimeter of a serving platter. In a large bowl, toss the sliced red and green cabbages with half the vinaigrette dressing. Mound this mixture in the center of the serving platter and surround with potatoes, radishes, hard-boiled eggs, Gouda cheese, Gruyère cheese, and cold cuts. Drizzle remaining vinaigrette over the dish. Garnish with minced parsley and edible flowers. Serve chilled.

⚜

Tartelettes aux Lardons et aux Poireaux
Lardons and Leek Tartlets

Makes eight 4-inch tartlets

2 cups flour
1 teaspoon salt
5 ounces unsalted butter, cubed
¼ cup ice water
5 ounces lardons
   (see Note page 46)
2 medium leeks
2 eggs, at room temperature

4 ounces goat cheese,
   at room temperature
3 ounces ricotta cheese,
   at room temperature
½ cup light cream
¾ teaspoon grated nutmeg
½ teaspoon salt

In a large bowl, combine the flour and salt. Pour onto a large work surface and create a well in the center. To this, add the cubes of butter. Work the ingredients together using your fingers until the mixture resembles coarse bread crumbs. Add ¼ cup ice water, one tablespoon at a time, and continue working the mixture until thoroughly incorporated. Form the mixture into a lump and knead with the palm of your hand for 10 to 15 seconds. Shape the dough, called *pâte brisée*, into a disk, cover with plastic wrap, and refrigerate for at least one hour or overnight.

Remove the dough from the refrigerator, slice into 8 wedges of equal size, and shape each one into a ball. On a lightly floured work surface, roll these into rounds 4½ inches in diameter. Transfer one round of dough to a 4-inch tartlet pan and gently mold it onto the bottom and sides. With a paring knife, trim the dough that extends over the rim and prick the bottom of the dough with the tines of a fork. Continue in this manner with the remaining seven rounds of dough. Set the tartlet pans aside.

In a small skillet, cook the lardons until crisp. Transfer to a plate lined with a paper towel to drain. Reserve the fat in the skillet.

Preheat the oven to 425 degrees F.

Trim and discard the leeks' roots and the upper half of their dark green leaves. Cut the remaining leaves and stems in half lengthwise and coarsely chop. Place the chopped leeks in a colander and rinse under running water to remove any traces of soil. Transfer them to the same skillet used for the lardons and cook the leeks until soft. Set aside.

In a medium bowl, beat the eggs and add the goat cheese, ricotta cheese, light cream, nutmeg, and salt. Mix until smooth and combine with the leeks and half of the lardons. Spoon equal amounts of this filling into the tartlet pans and garnish with remaining lardons. Bake for 20 to 25 minutes. Serve warm or at room temperature.

Tarte à l'Oignon
Onion Tart

SERVES 6

2 cups flour
1 teaspoon salt
5 ounces unsalted butter
¼ cup ice water
2 eggs
1 cup sour cream
½ cup whole milk
1 teaspoon Dijon mustard

1 cup shredded Gruyère cheese
⅛ teaspoon nutmeg
1½ pounds onions, thinly sliced
½ teaspoon salt
¼ teaspoon freshly ground
    black pepper
2 tablespoons all-purpose flour

In a large bowl, combine the flour and salt. Pour onto a large work surface and create a well in the center. Cube 4 ounces of the butter and work into the dry ingredients with your fingers. Add ¼ cup ice water, one tablespoon at a time, and continue working the mixture until it resembles coarse bread crumbs. Form into a lump and knead for 10 to 15 seconds before shaping into a disk. Cover the dough, called *pâte brisée*, with plastic wrap and refrigerate for at least one hour or overnight.

Preheat the oven to 425 degrees F.

In a medium mixing bowl, lightly beat the eggs and stir in the sour cream, milk, mustard, shredded Gruyère, and nutmeg. Set aside.

In a large skillet over medium heat, melt the remaining butter and cook the onions with the salt and the pepper, stirring occasionally, until soft, 7 to 8 minutes. Sprinkle with the flour and continue stirring until the onions turn golden, 3 to 4 minutes. Combine with the egg/sour-cream mixture.

Grease a 9-inch pie pan. Remove the dough from the refrigerator. On a lightly floured work surface, roll it into a round a little larger than the pie pan. Transfer the round to the pie pan and gently mold the dough onto the bottom and sides. With a paring knife, trim the dough that extends over the rim and prick the bottom with the tines of a fork. Set aside.

Pour the onion/egg mixture into the pie pan. Bake until the tart is puffy and golden brown, 30 to 35 minutes. Cool for 10 minutes before serving.

Flammekueche/Tarte Flambée
Alsatian Flatbread

MAKES ONE FLAT BREAD

1¼ cups all-purpose flour,
    divided use

2 teaspoons sea salt

3 tablespoons water

1 tablespoon vegetable oil

5 ounces lardons
    (see Note page 46)

1 large Spanish onion,
    very thinly sliced

3 ounces Boursin or other soft,
    herb-flavored cheese

⅓ cup crème fraîche

¼ teaspoon grated nutmeg

In a medium bowl, combine 1 cup of the flour and the salt. In increments, add the water and the vegetable oil and mix with your fingers until the dough stiffens. Sprinkle the remaining ¼ cup of flour onto a large work surface. Gently knead the dough until it becomes smooth. Over-kneading will cause the dough to lose elasticity. Cover with a clean towel and let the dough rest for one hour at room temperature.

In a small skillet over medium heat, cook the lardons until crisp. Transfer to a plate lined with a paper towel to drain. In the same skillet, cook the sliced onion until golden. Set aside.

Preheat the oven to 450 degrees F.

On the floured work surface, roll the dough into an 8-inch x 10-inch oval and transfer to a baking sheet lined with parchment paper.

In a bowl, mix the Boursin cheese with the crème fraîche and nutmeg. Using a spatula, spread the mixture over the dough. Top with the sliced onions, lardons, and a light sprinkling of salt.

Bake for 8 to 10 minutes, watching carefully so the edges of the crust don't burn. Serve hot or warm.

Sidebar: In my great-grandmother's day, *Flammekueche* or *Tarte flambée* was an inexpensive mid-morning snack purchased fresh from the oven at the local *boulangerie*. In recent years, the thin, pizza-like flat bread topped with onions, lardons, and cheese has become a favorite at bistros all over France.

Crêpes aux Champignons et au Jambon
Mushroom and Ham Crêpes

SERVES 6

7 tablespoons unsalted butter, divided use

1 cup milk

½ cup water

3 eggs

1 cup plus 1 tablespoon all-purpose flour, divided use

1¼ teaspoons salt

10 ounces button mushrooms, wiped clean and diced

½ cup finely diced ham

¼ teaspoon freshly ground black pepper

2 cups prepared tomato sauce

4 large Portobello mushrooms, wiped clean and sliced

½ cup grated Gruyère cheese

Preheat the oven to 400 degrees F.

Prepare the crêpes. In a small saucepan over low heat, melt 3 tablespoons of the butter. Pour it into a blender and add the milk, water, eggs, 1 cup of the flour, and ½ teaspoon of the salt. Blend until smooth and set the batter aside.

Over medium heat, lightly grease a crêpe pan. Pour in ⅓ cup of the batter and swirl to cover the bottom of the pan. Cook until the underside of the crêpe is golden brown, 2 to 3 minutes. Using a spatula, flip the crêpe over and cook for another 1 to 2 minutes. Continue in this manner with the remaining crêpes and stack on a dinner plate. Cover with plastic wrap and set aside.

In a medium skillet over medium heat, melt 3 tablespoons of the butter. Add the button mushrooms and cook until golden brown. Add the ham and sprinkle evenly with 1 tablespoon of flour, salt, and pepper. Add ⅓ cup of the tomato sauce, heat through, and set aside.

Spread ⅓ cup of the tomato sauce over the bottom of a 9-inch x 9-inch baking dish. Set the crêpes on a large flat surface and lightly spread each one with tomato sauce. Spoon equal amounts of the mushroom/ham mixture in the center of each crêpe and fold over the sides to enclose the filling. Set the crêpes snugly into the baking dish.

⚜

In a small skillet, melt the remaining butter and cook the sliced Portobello mushrooms until golden. Spoon the remaining tomato sauce over the crêpes in the baking dish and sprinkle with the grated Gruyère. Bake until bubbly and brown, 10 to 15 minutes. Garnish with the slices of Portobello mushrooms and serve.

Oeufs Brouillés
Scrambled Eggs

SERVES 4

8 organic, free-range eggs
2 tablespoons light cream
½ teaspoon salt
¼ teaspoon freshly ground black
 pepper

½ teaspoon dried tarragon leaves,
 crushed
3 tablespoons unsalted butter,
 divided use
¼ cup grated Gruyère cheese

In a medium bowl, beat the eggs and stir in the cream, salt, pepper, and tarragon.

In a medium skillet over medium heat, melt 2 tablespoons of the butter. Add the egg/cream mixture and lower the heat. Stir slowly and continuously while adding the Gruyère cheese, in increments, until the eggs are creamy and moist. Stir in the remaining pat of butter before serving.

Strudel Rouge et Vert
Red and Green Cabbage Strudel

MAKES TWO 10-INCH STRUDELS

1 (16-ounce) package frozen filo dough

4 ounces lardons (see Note page 46)

5 ounces red cabbage, diced

5 ounces green cabbage, diced

½ teaspoon fennel seeds

1 teaspoon salt

¼ teaspoon freshly ground black pepper

8 ounces unsalted butter

⅓ cup bread crumbs

Thaw the package of filo dough for 2 hours at room temperature or overnight in the refrigerator. Remove four sheets of dough, return the rest to the package, and refrigerate for another use. Transfer the four sheets of filo to a flat surface and cover with a damp towel to prevent drying. Set aside.

In a medium skillet over medium heat, brown the lardons until crisp. Add the diced red cabbage, diced green cabbage, and fennel seeds. Cover and cook over low heat until cabbage softens, 10 to 15 minutes. Season with salt and pepper and set aside.

Preheat the oven to 400 degrees F.

In a small pan over low heat, melt the butter and set aside. With a pastry brush, generously paint one sheet of filo with melted butter. Cover with a second layer of filo and repeat the process. Sprinkle with half of the bread crumbs. With the long side of the layered filo dough facing you, spread half the cabbage mixture along the bottom edge and 2½ inches in from each end. Fold the sides of the filo over the cabbage and roll up the bottom edge, brushing with more melted butter as you go. Proceed in this manner with the remaining two sheets of filo dough for the second strudel.

Carefully transfer the two rolls of filo to a baking sheet lined with parchment paper. Bake until golden, 20 to 25 minutes. Cool for 5 to 6 minutes. Cut the strudels on the diagonal and serve.

⚜

Choux aux Crevettes
Curried Shrimp Puffs

MAKES ABOUT 12 PUFFS

3 cups water, divided use
½ cup white wine
1 small carrot, peeled
    and thinly sliced
½ small onion studded with
    2 cloves
1 bouquet garni (see Note)
1½ teaspoons salt, divided use
¾ pound fresh unshelled shrimp
12 tablespoons unsalted butter,
    divided use

1⅓ cups whole milk, divided use
2 cups all-purpose flour,
    divided use
3 eggs, at room temperature
1 cup grated Gruyère cheese,
    divided use
¼ teaspoon freshly ground
    black pepper
1 teaspoon mild curry powder

To make the poaching stock (court bouillon) for the shrimp: in a medium saucepan over medium heat, bring 2½ cups of water, ½ cup of white wine, the carrot, onion studded with cloves, bouquet garni, and ½ teaspoon salt to a boil. To this stock, add the unshelled shrimp and boil until they turn pink, about 3 minutes. With a slotted spoon, transfer the shrimp to a bowl, let cool, and shell. Return the shrimp shells to the poaching liquid, add the remaining teaspoon of salt, and simmer for another 20 to 25 minutes. Discard the shells and the bay leaf. Strain the poaching liquid through a fine-mesh sieve and refrigerate. Cut the shrimp into small pieces and set aside.

Preheat the oven to 425 degrees F.

In a heavy bottom saucepan, bring 8 tablespoons of butter, ½ cup water, and ⅓ cup of the whole milk to a boil. Add 1¾ cups of flour, all at once. Using a wooden spoon, mix vigorously until the dough (what the French call pâte à choux) is smooth and separates from the sides of the pan. Remove from the heat and, while continuing to mix, add the eggs, one at a time, until each is fully incorporated. To this mixture, blend in ⅓ cup of the grated Gruyère cheese.

Line a small baking sheet with parchment paper. Spoon ¼-cup portions of pâte à choux onto the parchment paper, 2 inches apart. Bake until the puffs are golden, about 15 minutes. Reduce the heat to 325 degrees F and bake for another 15 minutes. Do **not** open the oven door while baking. Turn off the oven and leave the door ajar to allow the puffs to dry out for another 20 to 25 minutes. Remove from the oven to let them cool completely.

With a sharp knife, cut each puff horizontally to create a bowl and a cap. Set aside.

Meanwhile, in a medium saucepan over medium heat, melt the remaining 4 tablespoons of butter. Thoroughly blend in the remaining ¼ cup of flour. Add the remaining cup of milk, all at once, and cook, stirring continuously, until the mixture thickens, 3 to 4 minutes. Add ½ teaspoon of salt, pepper, curry powder, remaining grated Gruyère, and the pieces of shrimp. Stir to blend. Fill the puff bowls with the Gruyère/shrimp mixture and top with their corresponding caps. Serve warm or at room temperature.

Note: A bouquet garni is composed of aromatic herbs such as fresh or dried rosemary, thyme, and tarragon. Commercially prepared bouquets garnis are available in specialty stores or online.

Potage de Pommes de Terre à l'Oseille
Leek and Potato Soup with Sorrel

SERVES 4

3 medium leeks

4 cups chicken broth

1 pound small new potatoes, washed, peeled, and quartered

1 small onion, diced

8 leaves sorrel, chopped

1 teaspoon salt

¼ teaspoon white pepper

1 cup light cream

Croutons, for serving

Trim and discard the leeks' roots and upper half of their dark green leaves. Cut the remaining leaves and stems in half, lengthwise, and coarsely chop. Place the chopped leeks in a colander and rinse thoroughly under running water to remove any traces of soil. Set aside.

In a large saucepan over medium heat, bring the chicken broth to a low boil. Add the leeks, potatoes, onion, and three-quarters of the sorrel. Cook, covered, until the potatoes are tender, 15 to 20 minutes. Remove from the heat and let cool for 10 minutes. In a blender or food processor, in increments, puree the broth and vegetables until smooth and season with salt and pepper. Return to the saucepan, cover, and simmer for 8 to 10 minutes. Add cream, stirring occasionally, and heat through but do **not** boil.

To serve, ladle the soup into individual serving bowls and sprinkle with the remaining chopped sorrel and croutons. Serve hot or cold.

Sidebar: My great-grandmother would have used a hand-operated *moulin à légumes* (a food mill) to purée her vegetables.

Chapter Two

Vegetables and Sides

Galette de Pommes de Terre
Potato Galette

Petits Pois Bonne Femme
Green Peas with Mint and Wilted Lettuce

Endives Gratinées au Jambon
Ham-Wrapped Belgian Endives

Gratin Dauphinois
Potato Gratin

Chou Rouge à l'Alsacienne
Red Cabbage Alsatian-style

Haricots Verts Persillade
Green Beans with Parsley and Garlic

⚜

Galette de Pommes de Terre
Potato Galette

Serves 2

3 medium russet potatoes, peeled and grated (about 2 cups)
1 medium sweet potato, peeled and grated (about 1 cup)
1 medium Spanish onion, grated
2 eggs
1½ teaspoons salt
¼ teaspoon freshly ground black pepper
2 tablespoons plain bread crumbs
2 tablespoons unsalted butter
Crème fraîche, for serving

Using a clean towel, squeeze out and discard as much liquid from the grated vegetables as possible and set aside.

In a large bowl, lightly beat the eggs and thoroughly blend in the salt, pepper, bread crumbs, and drained vegetables.

In a 7-inch cast-iron skillet over medium-high heat, melt the butter. Swirl to coat the sides. Spread the vegetable/egg mixture evenly in the skillet. Cook until the bottom of the galette turns golden brown, 10 to 15 minutes. Carefully invert it onto a plate and slide it back into the skillet. Continue cooking over medium-high heat until the bottom turns golden brown, another 8 to 10 minutes. Transfer to a serving platter and serve warm with a dollop of crème fraîche.

Petits Pois Bonne Femme
Green Peas with Mint and Wilted Lettuce

SERVES 4

8 pearl onions, peeled
(see Note)
2 tablespoons diced lardons
(see Note page 46)
2 pounds fresh petite peas,
shelled
2 tablespoons water

4 whole leaves of butter lettuce,
washed and dried
6 fresh mint leaves, divided use
A pinch of granulated sugar
½ teaspoon salt
⅛ teaspoon freshly ground
black pepper

In a medium skillet over medium heat, cook the pearl onions and the lardons until the lardons are crisp. Drain most of the fat. Add the peas and the water. Cover and cook until the peas are soft, 8 to 10 minutes. Add the lettuce leaves, 4 of the mint leaves, sugar, salt, and pepper. Cook until the lettuce wilts. Chop the remaining mint leaves and sprinkle over the peas. Serve hot.

Note: To peel pearl onions, parboil them in a pan of boiling water for 2 to 3 minutes. Transfer them to a bowl of ice water to cool. Drain and peel.

Endives Gratinées au Jambon
Ham-Wrapped Belgian Endives

SERVES 4

4 Belgian endives

4 ounces unsalted butter,
    divided use

3 tablespoons all-purpose flour

1 cup whole milk

1 cup grated Gruyère cheese,
    divided use

8 slices smoked ham

Preheat the oven to 375 degrees F.

Wipe the endives with a soft, damp cloth. Do **not** soak them in water. Cut them in half, lengthwise, and set aside.

In a medium skillet over medium heat, melt 2 ounces of the butter. Brown the halved endives on both sides and set aside.

In a small saucepan, melt the remaining butter and stir in the flour. While stirring continuously, add the whole milk. Stir in ¾ cup of the Gruyère cheese until the sauce is thick enough to coat the back of a spoon.

Spread one quarter of the milk/cheese mixture over the bottom of an ovenproof dish large enough to accommodate the endive halves in a single layer. Wrap each half with a slice of ham and set in the baking dish. Cover the endives with the remaining cheese sauce and grated Gruyère. Bake until bubbly and brown, 20 to 25 minutes. Serve hot.

Gratin Dauphinois
Potato Gratin

SERVES 6

2 pounds russet potatoes
1 cup light cream
1 cup whole milk
2 garlic cloves, divided use
6 tablespoons unsalted butter,
    divided use

2 tablespoons all-purpose flour,
    divided use
1 teaspoon salt, divided use
½ teaspoon white pepper,
    divided use
½ teaspoon grated nutmeg,
    divided use
2 cups grated Gruyère cheese

Preheat the oven to 375 degrees F.

Peel and thinly slice the potatoes and pat them dry. Set aside.

In a medium saucepan over low heat, combine the light cream and the whole milk and bring to a simmer. Remove from the heat. Mince one of the garlic cloves and add to the milk/cream mixture.

Grease the bottom and sides of an 8-inch x 8-inch baking dish with 2 tablespoons of the butter. Cut the second garlic clove in half and rub it over the bottom and sides of the dish. Discard the garlic.

Cover the bottom of the baking dish with half of the potato slices and sprinkle with 1 tablespoon of flour. Add half of the milk/cream mixture and 2 tablespoons of butter. Over the top, sprinkle ½ teaspoon of salt, ¼ teaspoon of pepper, ¼ teaspoon of nutmeg, and half of the grated Gruyère cheese. Repeat this process with the remaining potato slices, flour, milk/cream mixture, butter, salt, pepper, nutmeg, and grated Gruyère.

Bake, uncovered, until potatoes are tender and the top is bubbly and golden brown, 50 to 55 minutes. Let stand 10 minutes before serving.

Chou Rouge à l'Alsacienne
Red Cabbage Alsatian-style

SERVES 4

4 tablespoons vegetable oil, divided use

12 pearl onions, parboiled and peeled (see Note page 73)

4 beef sausages such as *knockwurst*, cooked and sliced

1 medium Spanish onion, peeled and thinly sliced

1 small head red cabbage, cored and thinly sliced

2 tart apples, peeled, cored, and thinly sliced

1 teaspoon fennel seeds

½ cup balsamic vinegar

1 teaspoon salt

¼ teaspoon freshly ground black pepper

In a medium skillet over medium heat, heat 2 tablespoons of the vegetable oil. Cook the pearl onions and one quarter of the sliced sausage until the onions turn golden brown, about 15 minutes. Reserve for garnish.

In a heavy pan over medium heat, heat the remaining vegetable oil. Add the remaining sliced sausage, Spanish onion, red cabbage, apples, fennel seeds, vinegar, salt, and pepper. Cover and cook over low heat, stirring occasionally, until the cabbage becomes soft, 40 to 45 minutes. Garnish with the reserved pearl-onion/sausage mixture. Serve hot.

Haricots Verts Persillade
Green Beans with Parsley and Garlic

Serves 4

10 ounces French *haricots verts*, stringed and trimmed

3 medium new potatoes, peeled and cubed

6 pearl onions, parboiled and peeled (see Note page 73)

4 ounces diced lardons (see Note page 46)

1½ ounces veal demi-glace (see Note)

½ cup hot water

1 teaspoon salt

¼ teaspoon freshly ground black pepper

2 garlic cloves, finely minced

8 sprigs flat-leafed parsley, minced

In a medium saucepan filled with water, parboil the *haricots verts* until tender, 8 to 10 minutes. Drain and set aside. To the same pan, add fresh water and parboil the potatoes for 3 to 4 minutes. Drain and add to the green beans.

In a large skillet over medium heat, cook the pearl onions and the lardons until the lardons are crisp, 10 to 15 minutes. Drain most of the fat. With a slotted spoon, transfer the pearl-onion/lardons mixture to a small plate and reserve for garnish. In the same skillet over low heat, add the green beans and the potatoes.

Dissolve the demi-glace in ½ cup of hot water and add it to the green bean/potato mixture. Cover and cook until the potatoes turn soft, 8 to 10 minutes. Season with salt and pepper. Prepare a *persillade* by combining the minced garlic with the minced parsley. Transfer the *haricots verts* and potatoes to a serving dish and garnish with the pearl-onion/lardons mixture. Sprinkle with the *persillade* and serve hot.

Note: You can purchase veal demi-glace, a rich brown sauce made from veal stock and red wine, online or in specialty food stores.

Chapter Three • Main Dishes

Navarin d'Agneau aux Légumes
Lamb and Turnip Stew

Stufata
Beef and Vegetable Ragout in Red Wine

Côtes de Porc aux Légumes Rôties et aux Pomme Sautées
Pork Chops with Roasted Vegetables and Sautéed Apples

Pot-au-Feu
Beef and Vegetable Stew

Potée Alsacienne
Meat and Potato Casserole

Poulet au Vinaigre
Vinegar Chicken

Tourte Lorraine
Pork and Veal Pie

Spaetzle
Dumplings

Poulet au Riesling
Chicken in Riesling Wine

Escalopes de Veau aux Cerises
Veal Scallops with Fresh Cherries

Poisson au Vin Rouge
Fish in Red Wine

Choucroute à l'Alsacienne
Alsatian Sauerkraut

Magret de Canard aux Pruneaux
Duck Breast with Prunes

Civet de Lapin au Riesling
Rabbit Stew with Riesling Wine

Navarin d'Agneau aux Légumes
Lamb and Turnip Stew

SERVES 4

2 fennel bulbs

3 tablespoons unsalted butter

1½ pounds lamb shoulder,
    cut into chunks

1½ pounds leg of lamb,
    cut into chunks

12 pearl onions, parboiled and
    peeled (see Note page 73)

1 cup beef broth

1 beef bouillon cube

2 teaspoons fennel powder
    (see Note)

12 baby carrots, peeled

6 baby potatoes, peeled

6 baby turnips, peeled

1 cup peas

1½ teaspoons salt

½ teaspoon freshly ground
    black pepper

Crusty bread, for serving

Preheat the oven to 350 degrees F.

Trim the green fennel stalks an inch above the bulbs. Save the fronds and stems for another use—as a garnish, as an herb, or as a flavoring agent in soup stock. Cut one-half inch from the root ends. Place the bulbs on a flat surface and cut lengthwise, into thick wedges. Set aside.

In a Dutch oven over medium-high heat, melt the butter and brown the lamb shoulder, the leg of lamb, and the onions for 3 to 4 minutes. Add the beef broth, the bouillon cube, fennel wedges, and fennel powder. Cover tightly with a lid and transfer to the oven. Bake until the lamb is partially cooked, 45 to 50 minutes. Add the carrots, potatoes, and turnips and bake until the vegetables are tender, 30 to 35 minutes. Add the peas and heat through. Season with the salt and the pepper. Serve with crusty bread.

Note: Fennel powder is available in Middle Eastern markets. To make your own, toast 2 tablespoons of fennel seeds and process in a spice grinder.

Stufata
Beef and Vegetable Ragout in Red Wine

SERVES 4

2 pounds boneless beef sirloin

4 ounces diced lardons
   (see Note page 46)

2 dozen pearl onions, parboiled
   and peeled (see Note page 73)

8 baby carrots, peeled

6 baby turnips, peeled

3 cups Alsatian Pinot Noir wine

2 teaspoons salt

½ teaspoon freshly ground
   black pepper

1 bouquet garni (see Note page 65)

8 ounces whole cremini
   mushrooms, wiped clean

6 sprigs fresh parsley, minced

Crusty bread, for serving

With a paring knife, make deep incisions into the sirloin. Push the lardons into the slits using a ¼-inch wooden dowel or the blunt end of a chopstick.

Transfer the sirloin to a large bowl and add the pearl onions, carrots, turnips, wine, salt, pepper, and bouquet garni. Cover and marinate for at least one hour and drain, reserving the wine marinade separately from the meat and vegetables. Preheat the oven to 325 degrees F.

Transfer the sirloin and vegetables to a heavy Dutch oven that can go from oven to table. Add the mushrooms and 1 cup of the reserved wine marinade. Cover the pot with aluminum foil and a lid and transfer to the oven. Check the dish one hour into the cooking process and add more wine marinade if the meat seems dry. Bake until the meat is tender, 2 to 2½ hours. Discard the bouquet garni and the remaining marinade. Sprinkle with parsley and serve with crusty bread on the side.

Côtes de Porc aux Légumes Rôties et aux Pommes Sautées

Pork Chops with Roasted Vegetables and Sautéed Apples

Serves 2

1 pound small Brussels sprouts

12 pearl onions

4 tablespoons unsalted butter, divided use

1 garlic clove, peeled and sliced

12 baby potatoes, peeled

2 teaspoons salt, divided use

1 teaspoon freshly ground black pepper, divided use

3 Gala apples, cored, peeled, and thickly sliced

4 ½-inch thick, center-cut, bone-in pork chops, about 8 oz each

2 tablespoons vegetable oil

1 cup Riesling wine

1½ ounces chicken (or veal) demi-glace (see Note)

¼ cup crème fraîche

1 teaspoon fresh thyme leaves, finely chopped

Thyme sprigs, for garnish

Trim the Brussels sprouts of their thick outer leaves. In a large saucepan filled with water, parboil the Brussels sprouts, the pearl onions, and the potatoes for 3 to 4 minutes. Drain. Cool the pearl onions in cold water, peel, and set aside.

Preheat oven to 425 degrees F.

In a medium baking pan, add 2 tablespoons of the butter, garlic, Brussels sprouts, baby potatoes and pearl onions. Roast until nicely browned, 20 to 25 minutes. Turn off the oven. Season the vegetables with ¼ teaspoon salt and ⅛ teaspoon black pepper. Use aluminum foil to cover the vegetables and return them to the oven, with the door ajar, to keep warm.

On the stovetop, in a skillet over medium heat, melt 2 tablespoons of butter and cook the apples until soft and lightly browned, 20 to 25 minutes. Season with ¼ teaspoon of salt and ⅛ teaspoon of black pepper. Cover and transfer to the oven to keep warm.

Warm four serving plates in the oven.

Dry the pork chops with paper towels. Sprinkle the chops with equal amounts of the remaining salt and pepper. In a large cast-iron skillet over high heat, heat 2 tablespoons of vegetable oil. When the oil begins to smoke, set the pork chops in the skillet. Turn them over every minute for 4 minutes. Immediately transfer the chops to the warm serving plates and return to the oven.

Meanwhile, reduce the heat in the cast-iron skillet to medium and deglaze the pan with ½ cup of Riesling wine and cook until reduced by half. Add the demi-glace and whisk until dissolved. Lower the heat and stir in the crème fraîche and the finely chopped thyme. Transfer the sauce to a serving bowl.

To serve, surround the pork chops with equal amounts of roasted vegetables and sautéed apples. Drizzle demi-glace sauce over the chops and garnish with sprigs of thyme.

Note: You can purchase containers of chicken (or veal) demi-glace in specialty food stores and online.

Pot-au-Feu
Beef and Vegetable Stew

SERVES 6

2 medium leeks
8 cups water
10 beef short ribs
1 Spanish onion,
    peeled and left whole
2 whole cloves
1 garlic clove, peeled
10 sprigs parsley,
    tied with cotton string
2 bay leaves
4 small red potatoes,
    peeled, and quartered
3 medium carrots, peeled
    and sliced

2 small turnips, peeled
    and quartered
3 green onions, trimmed of tops
    and sliced
4 ribs celery, cut into 2-inch pieces
1 small Savoy cabbage,
    trimmed and cut into wedges
2 teaspoons salt
½ teaspoon freshly ground
    black pepper
Dijon mustard, for serving
Horseradish sauce, for serving
Cornichon-style pickles,
    for serving

Trim and discard the leeks' roots and upper half of their dark green leaves. Cut the remaining leaves and stems in half, lengthwise, and coarsely chop. Place in a colander and rinse thoroughly under running water to remove any traces of soil. Set aside.

In a soup pot over medium heat, bring the leeks, water, short ribs, Spanish onion, cloves, garlic, parsley, and bay leaves to a low boil. Simmer for 1 hour. Add the potatoes, carrots, turnips, green onions, celery, cabbage, salt, and pepper. Simmer until the meat is fork tender, an additional 45 to 50 minutes. Skim off the fat. Discard the parsley sprigs, onion, cloves, and bay leaves.

With a slotted spoon, transfer the meat and the vegetables to a platter. Serve with the broth, mustard, horseradish, and cornichons on the side.

Potée Alsacienne
Meat and Potato Casserole

SERVES 6

1 medium leek

1½ pounds boneless beef chuck roast, trimmed and cut into 1½-inch pieces

2 pounds boneless lamb shoulder, trimmed and cut into 1½-inch pieces

4 small Spanish onions, sliced, divided use

4 garlic cloves, peeled and sliced, divided use

¼ cup minced parsley

2 bay leaves

2 medium carrots, thinly sliced

2 cups Riesling wine

3 pounds russet potatoes

3 teaspoons salt, divided use

1½ teaspoons freshly ground black pepper

Six 4-inch sprigs fresh rosemary, divided use

Six 2-inch sprigs fresh thyme, minced

¼ cup vegetable oil

Two hours ahead, trim and discard the leek's roots and upper half of the dark green leaves. Slice the stem into ½-inch rounds. Place them in a colander and rinse thoroughly under running water to remove any traces of soil.

In a large bowl, place the pieces of beef and lamb. Add the leeks, half of the sliced onions, half of the sliced garlic, the parsley, bay leaves, sliced carrots, and Riesling wine. Refrigerate for 2 hours. Drain and discard marinade, reserving vegetables and meat separately.

Peel and thinly slice the potatoes. Set aside in a bowl of water to prevent discoloration.

Preheat the oven to 325 degrees F.

Strip the leaves from 2 rosemary sprigs, reserving the remaining sprigs for garnish. Spread a third of the sliced potatoes over the bottom of a *Römertopf* (clay baking dish) and cover with half of the vegetables, marinated meat, salt, pepper, rosemary leaves, and thyme. Repeat this process with a second layer of sliced potatoes and the remaining vegetables, meat, salt, pepper, rosemary leaves, and thyme. Top with the remaining potatoes and drizzle with the vegetable oil. Seal the *Römertopf* with aluminum foil and cover with a lid. Transfer to the center rack of the oven and bake for 2 to 2½ hours. Remove the lid and foil and place under the broiler until the potatoes are browned, 3 to 4 minutes. Discard the bay leaves. Garnish the dish with the reserved sprigs of rosemary and serve..

Poulet au Vinaigre
Vinegar Chicken

SERVES 4

6 tablespoons unsalted butter,
   divided use

5 chicken thighs

5 chicken legs

½ cup diced onion

12 pearl onions, parboiled and
   peeled (see Note page 73)

1 cup apple cider vinegar

½ cup Riesling wine

15 garlic cloves, unpeeled

½ cup diced tomatoes

2 medium carrots,
   peeled and sliced

12 button mushrooms

Bouquet garni (see page 65)

2 tablespoons tomato paste

½ cup chicken broth

1 chicken bouillon cube

⅓ cup crème fraîche

Chopped chives, for garnish

Crusty bread, for serving

Preheat the oven to 375 degrees F.

In a medium cast-iron pan over medium heat, melt 4 tablespoons of the butter. Brown the chicken thighs and legs. Add the diced onion and pearl onions and cook until lightly browned.

Deglaze the pan with the vinegar and the Riesling wine. Add the unpeeled garlic cloves, diced tomatoes, carrots, mushrooms, and bouquet garni. Cover and bake until the chicken is tender, 40 to 45 minutes.

With a slotted spoon, transfer the chicken to a bowl and keep warm. Discard the bouquet garni. Transfer the garlic cloves to a small plate and squeeze the pulp from the skins. Discard the skins. Add the garlic pulp, tomato paste, broth, and bouillon cube to the pan. Cook over medium heat, stirring occasionally, until the broth reduces by one third. Remove from the heat and stir in the crème fraîche and remaining butter. Return the chicken to the pan and heat through. Sprinkle with chopped chives and serve with crusty bread.

Tourte Lorraine
Pork and Veal Pie

SERVES 6

1 pound lean, boned, center-cut pork chop, cut into ½-inch cubes

½ pound boned veal, cut into ½-inch cubes

½ cup Riesling wine

1 whole clove

2 bay leaves

2 shallots, minced

¼ cup chopped flat-leaf parsley

2 garlic cloves, peeled and sliced

¼ cup vegetable oil

2 teaspoons salt, divided use

½ teaspoon freshly ground black pepper, divided use

1 teaspoon finely minced rosemary leaves

Leaves from 2 sprigs of thyme

2 sheets puff pastry, thawed

3 eggs, divided use

½ cup crème fraîche

In a large bowl, combine the pork and veal with the Riesling wine, whole clove, bay leaves, shallots, parsley, and sliced garlic. Cover and marinate in the refrigerator for 2 hours. Reserve the meat and marinade separately. Discard the whole clove.

Preheat the oven to 325 degrees F.

In a medium cast-iron baking pan over medium heat, heat the vegetable oil and brown the meat for 3 to 4 minutes. Add ½ cup of the marinade and discard the rest. Cover the pan, transfer to the oven, and bake until the meat is fork tender, 1 to 1½ hours. Remove from the oven. Discard the bay leaf. Using a slotted spoon, transfer the meat to a cutting board and coarsely dice. In a bowl, combine the diced meat with 1 teaspoon of the salt, ¼ teaspoon of the pepper, the rosemary, and the thyme. Set aside.

Increase the oven temperature to 425 degrees F.

On a lightly floured work surface, roll out a sheet of puff pastry to 13½ inches in diameter and mold it onto the bottom and sides of a straight-sided, 9-inch pie pan (2 inches deep). Allow extra dough to hang over the edges. With a paring knife, trim away excess and save for decoration. Spoon the diced meat into the pie pan.

Roll out the second sheet of puff pastry to 10 inches in diameter. With your finger, wet the dough-covered rim of the pan and quickly top with the second sheet of puff pastry. Seal using the tines of a fork. Again, trim excess dough and save for decoration. Cut a 1-inch opening in the center of the top sheet.

On the floured work surface, roll out the excess dough and cut out decorative shapes with a cookie cutter. Set these aside. Beat one of the eggs and, with a pastry brush, apply some of the egg wash to the puff pastry. Top with the cookie cutouts and brush with the remaining egg wash. Transfer to the oven and bake for 30 minutes. Meanwhile, prepare a savory custard (called *migaine*) by beating together the remaining eggs, crème fraîche, the remaining salt, and the remaining pepper. Set aside.

Remove the pie from the oven and lower the temperature to 350 degrees F. Pour the *migaine* through the opening in the top crust and gently swirl. Return the pie to the oven and bake until the *migaine* has set, 10 to 15 minutes. Serve warm.

Spaetzle Dumplings

SERVES 4

2 cups all-purpose flour
2 teaspoons salt, divided use
1 teaspoon minced parsley
4 eggs, at room temperature

⅓ cup whole milk
4 tablespoons unsalted butter
4 garlic cloves, minced

In a large bowl, combine the flour, 1 teaspoon of the salt, and the parsley. Set aside.

In another bowl, combine the eggs and the milk. Add to the flour mixture and stir until it achieves the consistency of a thick pancake batter. Cover and let rest for 30 minutes.

Bring a large pot of water and the remaining salt to a boil. Spoon a portion of the *spaetzle* batter into a ricing implement and slowly extrude the batter into the pot of boiling water. Diminutive dumplings will float to the surface. Let them boil for 3 to 4 minutes and, using a slotted spoon, transfer them to a colander to drain. Rinse under running water and return the *spaetzle* to the colander to drain a second time.

Repeat the process with the remaining batter.

In a skillet over medium heat, melt the butter with the garlic. Add the *spaetzle* and heat through. Keep warm until ready to serve—with dishes like *Poulet au Riesling* (see page 94), *Poulet au Vinaigre* (see page 89), or *Pot-au-Feu* (see page 85).

Poulet au Riesling
Chicken in Riesling Wine

SERVES 4

4 chicken legs
4 chicken thighs
½ cup flour
1 teaspoon salt
¼ teaspoon pepper
4 tablespoons unsalted butter,
    divided use
2 tablespoons vegetable oil
2 cloves garlic, minced
3 shallots, very finely diced
2 medium carrots, peeled and
    sliced thinly on the diagonal

1 half-ounce package of dried
    chanterelle mushrooms,
    plumped in warm water,
    and drained
1 bay leaf
1½ cups dry Riesling wine,
    divided use
½ cup chicken broth
1 cup crème fraiche
Parsley, finely chopped,
    for garnish
Spaetzle (see page 93)

Preheat oven to 375 degrees F.

Pat dry the chicken. Set aside.

Place the flour, salt, and pepper in a paper bag. Add the chicken and shake to coat. Set aside.

In a heavy pan or skillet, melt the butter and the oil over medium heat. Brown the chicken on all sides, turning them over with tongs for 5 to 6 minutes. Transfer them to a Dutch oven or heavy baking dish that can go from oven to table. Add the garlic, shallots, carrots, chanterelle mushrooms, bay leaf, and 1 cup of the Riesling wine. Transfer to the oven and bake until the chicken is tender, 50 to 55 minutes. Discard the bay leaf. Using a slotted spoon, transfer the chicken and vegetables to a serving dish and keep warm. Let the sauce continue to simmer in the pan.

To the sauce, add the remaining Riesling wine and the chicken broth. Increase the heat to medium-high and reduce the sauce by a third.

Lower the heat and, in increments, add the crème fraîche to the simmering sauce. Do **not** boil. Pour the sauce over the chicken and vegetables. Garnish with the carrots and parsley and serve over *spaetzle* dumplings (see page 93).

Escalopes de Veau aux Cerises
Veal Scallops with Fresh Cherries

SERVES 4

1 tablespoon cornstarch

¾ cup chicken broth,
    divided use

2 tablespoons honey

2 tablespoons balsamic
    vinegar

1 pound fresh cherries, pitted

2 teaspoons salt, divided use

½ teaspoon freshly ground
    black pepper, divided use

2 eggs

1 cup plain bread crumbs

8 veal scallops

8 tablespoons unsalted butter

5 ounces lardons
    (see Note page 46)

1 onion, finely sliced

1 small red cabbage
    (1 to 1½ pounds), cored
    and thinly sliced

Combine the cornstarch in 2 tablespoons of chicken broth. Set aside. In a medium saucepan over medium heat, combine the remaining broth, honey, and balsamic vinegar. Stir to blend. Add the cornstarch/broth mixture and stir until the sauce begins to thicken. Add the cherries and cook until they soften, 8 to 10 minutes. Season with 1 teaspoon of the salt and ¼ teaspoon of the pepper. Keep warm in the oven.

Beat the eggs in a shallow plate. In another shallow plate, combine the bread crumbs and the remaining salt and pepper.

Lightly pound the scallops, coat them with beaten egg, and dredge them in the bread crumbs. In a large skillet over medium heat, melt the butter. Add the scallops and cook until brown, 4 to 5 minutes on each side. Drain on paper towels and keep warm in the oven.

In another skillet, cook the lardons and sliced onions until the onions begin to soften, 8 to 10 minutes. Drain most of the fat. Add the sliced cabbage. Cover and cook, stirring occasionally, until the cabbage is soft, 10 to 12 minutes.

To serve, mound one cup of the lardons/cabbage mixture onto each dinner plate. Top with a veal scallop, a few cherries, and a ladleful of cherry sauce.

⚜

Poisson au Vin Rouge
Fish in Red Wine

SERVES 2

3 cups court bouillon poaching
   stock, divided use (see Note)
1½ pounds filleted salmon or trout
1 medium leek
4 tablespoons unsalted butter,
   divided use
1 small onion, finely diced
1 tablespoon capers, drained
6 ounces sliced mushrooms

⅓ cup all-purpose flour
1 cup medium bodied red wine,
   such as Pinot Noir
1 teaspoon salt
¼ teaspoon freshly ground
   black pepper
4 ounces crème fraîche
Sorrel leaves, for garnish

In a medium saucepan over medium heat, bring 2 cups court bouillon to a simmer. Immerse the salmon (or trout) fillets and poach until the flesh turns opaque and flaky, 7 to 10 minutes, depending upon the thickness of the fillets. Using a slotted spatula, carefully transfer the fillets to a platter. Remove and discard the skin. Cover with aluminum foil and keep warm until serving. Strain and reserve the court bouillon.

Trim and discard the leek's roots and dark green leaves. Cut the stem into ½-inch rounds, place in a colander, and rinse under running water to remove any traces of soil. Set aside to drain.

In a heavy skillet over medium heat, melt 2 tablespoons of the butter and cook the diced onion, the leek rounds, and the capers until the onion turns golden. Add the sliced mushrooms and cook until soft. With a slotted spoon, transfer this leek/mushroom mixture to a bowl and set aside.

In the same skillet over medium heat, melt the remaining butter. Add the flour and stir until the mixture turns golden. Add the red wine and stir until the sauce thickens somewhat. While stirring, slowly add 1 cup of court bouillon. To this, add the leek/mushroom mixture and season with salt and pepper. Stir in the crème fraîche. Using the slotted spatula, gently set the fillets in this sauce and heat through, 4 to 5 minutes. Transfer to a serving dish and garnish with the sorrel leaves. Serve over *spaetzle* (see page 93).

Note: For the court bouillon poaching stock, in a medium saucepan over medium heat, bring 4 cups of water to a boil. Add 1¼ cups of white wine, ½ cup chopped leeks, 1 small onion (studded with 2 cloves), 2 or 3 juniper berries (available in fine food stores), 6 peppercorns, 2 bay leaves, a bouquet garni of parsley and thyme, and 2½ teaspoons salt. Reduce the heat and simmer for 45 to 50 minutes, periodically skimming off the froth that collects on the surface. Strain the court bouillon through a fine-mesh sieve into a large bowl. Whatever isn't used right away can be refrigerated or frozen. You can find sorrel at farmers' markets.

Sidebar: Atlantic salmon in their thousands once swam against the current of the Seine and its tributary, the Marne, to return to the spot where they were spawned. Today, relatively few do so because of once polluted water in the Seine and the construction of hydroelectric dams. With help from the French government, the fish are making a slow but steady recovery. Nevertheless, *La Fédération de la Marne pour la Pêche et la Protection du Milieu Aquatique* prohibits sportsmen from taking *Le Roi du Poisson* (The King of Fish). There are no such restrictions for trout, which continue to thrive in the Marne and in other rivers in the French region of *Le Grand Est*.

Choucroute à l'Alsacienne
Alsatian Sauerkraut

SERVES 6

20 ounces fresh sauerkraut,
    rinsed and drained
4 ounces diced lardons
    (see Note page 46)
1 Spanish onion, diced
2 garlic cloves, peeled
1 tart apple, cored, peeled,
    and cut into 1-inch cubes
8 small red potatoes,
    halved, boiled for 3 minutes,
    and drained

1 pound pork butt
1 (12-ounce) bottle of Alsatian
    or any light beer
6 juniper berries
2 tablespoons light brown sugar
1 cup beef broth
12 assorted German sausages
    (like uncured Bavarian
    bratwurst, weisswurst, and
    smoked knockwurst)
Grainy French mustard, for serving

Preheat the oven to 375 degrees F.

In a large saucepan over high heat, bring water to a boil and blanch the sauerkraut for 3 minutes. Drain and set aside.

In a skillet over medium heat, cook the lardons and diced onion, stirring occasionally, until the onion is soft, about 3 minutes. Drain most of the fat and set aside.

Rub the inside of a *Romertöpf* with garlic cloves and discard the cloves. Evenly distribute the lardons/onion mixture over the bottom. Add the sauerkraut, cubed apple, potatoes, pork butt, beer, juniper berries, brown sugar, and beef broth. Cover and bake until the pork is fork tender, 2½ to 3 hours. Discard the juniper berries and return the *Romertöpf* to the oven to keep warm.

Meanwhile, in a skillet over medium heat, brown the sausages. Slice the larger ones on the diagonal and leave the small ones whole. Transfer them to the oven to keep warm.

To serve, mound sauerkraut, apples, potatoes, and pork butt on a shallow platter. Garnish with the sausages. Serve hot, with mustard on the side.

Magret de Canard aux Pruneaux
Duck Breast with Prunes

SERVES 2

5 ounces pitted prunes
½ cup Pinot Noir wine
1 cup chicken broth
6 threads Spanish saffron, crushed
2 duck breasts, rinsed
	and patted dry
1½ teaspoons salt
2 tablespoons unsalted butter

1 teaspoon ground ginger
1 medium onion, diced
2 tablespoons honey
½ teaspoon freshly ground
	black pepper
1 tablespoon slivered almonds,
	toasted, for garnish

Soak the prunes in the Pinot Noir wine for 2 to 3 hours. Drain and set aside.

Meanwhile, warm the broth. Add the saffron and steep for 10 minutes. Set aside.

Lay the duck breasts on a work surface. With a sharp knife, make intersecting diagonal cuts (about 1 inch apart) through the skin and fatty layers, **without** slicing into the flesh. Lightly sprinkle the breasts with salt.

Preheat the oven to 400 degrees F.

In a heavy cast-iron skillet that goes from stovetop to oven, over medium heat, melt the butter with the ground ginger. Sear the breasts, scored side down, pressing them against the bottom of the pan until the skins start to curl and turn light brown. Reduce the heat to medium low and cook for another 10 to 12 minutes. Turn the breasts, scored side up and transfer the skillet to the preheated oven. Roast until the duck breasts are pink in the center (about 8 to 10 minutes) or their internal temperature reaches 135 to 140 degrees F on a meat thermometer. Remove from the oven. Transfer the duck breasts to a baking dish and keep warm.

Transfer the skillet (with the duck drippings) to the stove. Over medium heat, add the diced onions and cook until golden. Add the saffron broth, the prunes, and the honey. Cook, stirring occasionally, until the mixture thickens, 6 to 8 minutes. Season with the remaining salt and pepper. Keep warm in the oven.

Slice the duck breasts on the diagonal and arrange in a fan shape on individual dinner plates. Garnish with the honeyed prunes and toasted slivered almonds before serving.

Civet de Lapin au Riesling
Rabbit Stew with Riesling Wine

SERVES 4

One (2½ to 3 lb) rabbit, cut up
3 cups Riesling wine, divided use
2 sprigs dried thyme, divided use
2 bay leaves
4 peppercorns
3 tablespoons vegetable oil
2 whole onions, sliced
2 garlic cloves, peeled and sliced

1 carrot, peeled and sliced
4 tablespoons flour
1 slice calf liver (about 5 ounces), diced
1 ounce dried morel mushrooms, soaked and drained
2 teaspoons salt
¼ teaspoon pepper

The day before, marinate the rabbit with 2 cups of the wine, 1 sprig of thyme, the bay leaves, and the peppercorns. Cover and refrigerate.

Preheat oven to 350 degrees F.

Drain and reserve the rabbit marinade. In a heavy cast-iron pan over medium heat, heat the oil and brown the rabbit pieces on all sides. Transfer them to a plate.

In the same pan, add the onions, garlic, and sliced carrot. Sprinkle with flour and cook, stirring occasionally, until the onions are translucent, 8 to 10 minutes. Return the rabbit and marinade to the pan. Add the calf liver and the morels. Season with the salt, pepper, and the second sprig of thyme. Cover tightly and bake for 50 to 55 minutes. Remove the lid and let the sauce reduce for 10 to 15 minutes in the oven. Remove pan from the oven. Using a fork, coarsely mash the liver. Discard the bay leaves and serve.

Chapter Four

Desserts and Baked Goods

Clafoutis aux Cerises
Cherry Clafoutis

Saucisson au Chocolat
Chocolate Sausage

Cruchades de Maïs
Fried Cornmeal "Coins"

Gratin de Framboises
Raspberry Gratin

Mousse au Chocolat
Chocolate Mousse

Kalougat de Blanche
Chocolate Pudding Cake

Meringues à la Framboise
Meringues with Raspberry Coulis

Truffes au Chocolat
Chocolate Truffles

Biscuits à l'Avoine
Oat Flour Almond cookies

Macarons de Blanche
Blanche's Macaroons

Pain d'Epices
Spice Cake

**Crêpes à la Crème de Marrons
et Ganache**
Crêpes with Chestnut Cream
and Ganache

Crème Anglaise
Vanilla Custard

Flan à la Crème de Riz
Cream of Rice Flan

Crème Pâtissière
Pastry Cream

Croissants aux Amandes
Almond Crescents

Pets-de-Nonne
Choux Pastry Puffs

**Ile Flottante aux Amandes
Caramélisées**
Floating Island with
Caramelized Almonds

Pommes au Four
Baked Apples

Gâteau de Carottes
Carrot Cake

Bredele
Shortbread Cookies

Tartelettes au Fromage Blanc
Cheesecake Tartlets

Tarte aux Prunes
Plum Tart

Tarte aux Pommes
Apple Tart

**Pudding de Pain avec
Crème Anglaise**
Bread Pudding with Vanilla Custard

Zimmetkuchen
Cinnamon Coffee Cake
with Crème Fraîche

Beignets de Carnaval
Doughnuts for Carnaval

**Pudding de Riz aux Cerises
et Crème au Kirsch**
Rice Pudding with Cherries
and Kirsch Cream

Bûche de Noël
Yule Log

Caramel

Croquembouche
French Wedding Cake

Brioche
Alsatian Brioche

Biscuits aux Amandes
Almond Macaroon Cookies

Clafoutis aux Cerises
Cherry Clafoutis

SERVES 6

4 tablespoons unsalted butter, divided use
¾ cup granulated sugar, divided use
1 pound fresh cherries, stemmed and pitted

1¼ cups all-purpose flour
1 cup whole milk, warmed
3 eggs
¾ teaspoon almond extract
Powdered sugar, for dusting

Preheat the oven to 400 degrees F.

Using one tablespoon of the butter, grease the ramekins and sprinkle each one with one tablespoon of granulated sugar. Add two layers of cherries to each ramekin. Set aside.

In a medium bowl, combine the flour and remaining sugar. Whisk in the milk, eggs, and almond extract until smooth. Fill the ramekins with equal amounts of this mixture, about ⅔ cup per ramekin. Dot each one with half a tablespoon of butter.

Bake for 45 to 50 minutes or until set.

Dust the clafoutis with powdered sugar.

Serve warm or at room temperature.

Note: In France, the cherries in clafoutis are generally left unpitted.

Saucisson au Chocolat
Chocolate Sausage

Serves 6

10 ounces dark chocolate, broken into pieces
3½ ounces honey

1½ ounces unsalted butter
7 ounces chopped almonds
Dark cocoa powder, for dusting

Bring water to a boil in the lower container of a double boiler. Remove from the heat and, to the upper container, add the chocolate, honey, and butter. Stir until smooth. Fold in the chopped almonds.

Line a baking sheet with aluminum foil. Spread the chocolate/almond mixture onto the foil and, when cool to the touch, roll it into the shape of a sausage and refrigerate. To serve, dust with cocoa powder and cut the *saucisson* into slices. Store in the refrigerator for up to two weeks.

Cruchades de Maïs
Fried Cornmeal "Coins"

MAKES ABOUT 25

2 cups yellow cornmeal	3 tablespoons brandy
2 cups water	1 cup all-purpose flour,
2 cups whole milk	for dredging
1 teaspoon salt	Vegetable oil for frying
2 tablespoons granulated sugar	Honey, for drizzling

Pour the cornmeal into a bowl and add enough water to cover. Stir the mixture and discard any impurities that float to the surface. Drain the water and set aside.

In a medium saucepan over medium-high heat, bring the 2 cups of water and the milk to a low boil. Reduce heat to medium low and add the cornmeal, salt, sugar, and brandy. Stir continuously until the cornmeal mixture becomes thick enough to hold a spoon upright, 10 to 12 minutes.

Spoon the cornmeal mixture onto a 9-inch x 13-inch non-stick baking sheet and spread it out as evenly as possible with an offset spatula. Use a straight rolling pin to create a uniformly flat surface. Refrigerate for 1 to 2 hours.

Using a 2-inch cookie cutter, cut the chilled dough into rounds. Pour the flour onto a platter. Dredge the rounds and set them aside.

In a heavy pan or deep fat fryer, heat the oil to 350 degrees F. Fry the dredged rounds, a few at a time, until they are golden brown. Transfer the "coins" to a plate lined with paper towels to drain. Serve warm with honey on the side.

⚜

Gratin de Framboises
Raspberry Gratin

SERVES 8

12 ounces fresh raspberries
2 tablespoons Chambord
raspberry liqueur
4 eggs, at room temperature,
divided use

2 cups whole milk
2 teaspoons vanilla
½ cup granulated sugar
½ cup all-purpose flour

Reserve 16 raspberries for garnish. In a medium bowl, combine the rest of the berries with the Chambord raspberry liqueur and set aside.

Separate the eggs, saving the whites for another use.

In a medium saucepan over medium heat, warm the milk and the vanilla but do **not** boil. In a small bowl, whisk the egg yolks and the sugar until smooth. Add the flour and continue whisking. Slowly pour in half of the warm milk/vanilla mixture and whisk until smooth. Set aside.

Return the other half of the milk/vanilla mixture to the stove. Over low heat, stirring continuously, add the egg/sugar/flour mixture. Stir until lumps disappear and the mixture coats the back of a spoon. Press this warm custard through a sieve placed above a chilled bowl and set aside.

Divide the macerated raspberries equally among the eight ramekins and do the same with the custard. Broil until scorch marks begin to appear on the surface of the custard. Garnish with reserved raspberries and serve.

Mousse au Chocolat
Chocolate Mousse

SERVES 4

2 organic free-range eggs
(see Note)
2 tablespoons rum
4 ounces semi-sweet chocolate,
broken into pieces

½ teaspoon cream of tartar
2 teaspoons granulated sugar
½ cup heavy cream
Edible and/or candied flowers,
for garnish

Separate the eggs. In a medium bowl, beat the egg yolks with the rum. Reserve the whites.

Bring water to a boil in a double boiler. Remove from heat and add the chocolate to the upper container. Stir until smooth. Slowly incorporate the molten chocolate into the egg yolk/rum mixture. Set aside.

In a medium bowl, beat the egg whites and cream of tartar until soft peaks form. Add the sugar and continue beating until stiff peaks form. Set aside.

Whip the heavy cream until stiff peaks form. Using a spatula, gently fold in the whipped cream, then the beaten egg whites into the chocolate/rum/egg mixture. Spoon equal quantities of this mousse into four ramekins. Garnish with edible and/or candied flowers. Refrigerate until ready to serve.

Note: When using raw eggs, make sure they come from an organic, free-range source. Pregnant women and immunosuppressed patients should refrain from eating raw eggs. To pasteurize eggs, hold them for 3 to 5 minutes in water heated to 140–145 degrees F.

Kalougat de Blanche
Chocolate Pudding Cake

SERVES 6

9 tablespoons unsalted butter, divided use

7 ounces dark chocolate, broken into pieces

4 eggs, at room temperature

1 cup powdered sugar, sifted, divided use

¼ cup almond meal (Note p. 125)

2 teaspoons white vinegar

Crème anglaise (see page 131)

Kalougat pudding cake is best if prepared a day ahead.

Preheat the oven to 325 degrees F.

Using one tablespoon of the butter, grease the bottom and sides of an 8-inch, straight sided baking pan. Line the bottom with a round of parchment paper. Set aside.

In a double boiler over high heat, bring water to a boil. Remove from the heat and add the chocolate and the rest of the butter to the upper container. Stir the mixture until smooth. Set aside.

Separate the eggs. In a large bowl, beat the egg yolks with ¾ cup of the powdered sugar until the mixture forms thick ribbons. To this, in increments, add the almond meal and the chocolate/butter mixture. Set aside.

In another large bowl, beat the egg whites and vinegar until soft peaks form. Add the remaining ¼ cup of powdered sugar and continue beating until stiff peaks form. Fold this into the butter/chocolate/almond-meal mixture and pour the resultant batter into the pie pan. Set in a water bath in the oven. Bake until the cake is set, 45 to 50 minutes. Remove from the oven and cool on a rack for 10 minutes before unmolding. Peel away the parchment paper and return the *kalougat* to a rack to cool overnight.

To serve, pool warm crème anglaise onto each dessert plate. Cut the *kalougat* into six wedges and set one of these in the center of each plate.

Sidebar: Both the spelling of this dessert (*kalouga, kalougat,* or *kaluga*) and its origin were a mystery to me—until my friend and colleague, Greg Patent, also known as *The Baking Wizard*, pointed out that *Kalouga* resembled a *Torta Caprese*, a flourless chocolate cake originally from the island of Capri.

⚜

Meringues à la Framboise
Meringues with Raspberry Coulis

Makes 6

4 eggs, at room temperature, separated, divided use
⅛ teaspoon salt
¼ teaspoon cream of tartar
1⅓ cups granulated sugar, divided use

1 teaspoon apple cider vinegar
1 teaspoon vanilla
24 ounces fresh raspberries
⅓ cup water

Preheat the oven to 250 degrees F.

Cut out six 2½-inch rounds of parchment paper and space evenly on a baking sheet. Set aside.

In a large bowl, combine the egg whites with the salt and the cream of tartar. Save the yolks for another use. Beat the whites until soft peaks form. Add 1 cup of the sugar, one tablespoon at a time, and continue beating until stiff peaks form. Add the vinegar and beat for 2 minutes. Fold in the vanilla. Place a half cup of this mixture onto each parchment round on the baking sheet. Bake until the meringues harden, about 45 minutes. Turn off the oven and leave the door ajar. Let the meringues dry for 1 to 2 hours. Remove them from the oven and set aside to cool. Store in an airtight container.

To make the coulis: In a blender or food processor, puree half the raspberries with the water. Strain into a small saucepan. Over medium heat, add the remaining ⅓ cup sugar and cook, stirring occasionally, until the mixture reduces by a third, 15 to 20 minutes. Set aside to cool.

Top the meringues with the remaining raspberries, drizzle with coulis, and serve.

Truffes au Chocolat
Chocolate Truffles

MAKES 22 TO 24

2 eggs, at room temperature, separated, divided use
3 heaping tablespoons powdered sugar
1 teaspoon kirsch cherry brandy
4 ounces semi-sweet chocolate, broken into pieces

2 tablespoons heavy cream
4 ounces unsalted butter, at room temperature
1 cup dark cocoa powder
Fluted paper cups

In a medium bowl, lightly beat the yolks with the powdered sugar. Stir in the kirsch. Set aside. Save the whites for another use.

Bring water to a boil in a double boiler. Remove from the heat and add the chocolate, heavy cream, and butter to the upper container. Stir until smooth. Slowly incorporate this into the egg/sugar/kirsch mixture. Refrigerate until firm.

Form heaping teaspoons of the chilled chocolate mixture into ¾-inch balls and roll them on a plate covered with the cocoa powder. Place the truffles in fluted paper cups. Refrigerate in a covered container.

Biscuits à l'Avoine
Oat Flour Almond Cookies

MAKES ABOUT 2 DOZEN

2 cups oat flour (see Note)
6½ ounces dark brown sugar
2 teaspoons baking soda
½ teaspoon salt
4 ounces unsalted butter, cubed,
   at room temperature

1 egg, at room temperature,
   separated, divided use
⅓ cup crushed almonds

In a large bowl, combine the oat flour, brown sugar, baking soda, and salt. To this, add the cubes of butter and the egg yolk. Work the ingredients together using your fingers until the mixture resembles coarse bread crumbs.

In a medium bowl, beat the egg white until stiff peaks form and fold into the oat-flour/yolk/butter mixture. Work with your hands until the dough achieves a uniform consistency. Transfer to a work surface generously sprinkled with oat flour and roll into a cylindrical shape, about 2 inches in diameter. Wrap in parchment paper and refrigerate until firm.

Preheat the oven to 375 degrees F.

Line a cookie sheet with parchment paper.

Remove the dough from the refrigerator and cut into ¼-inch-thick rounds. Set them 2 inches apart on the cookie sheet and press some crushed almonds into each round. Bake for 10 to 12 minutes. Cool on a rack and store in an airtight container.

Note: Oat flour is available in specialty markets and health food stores.

Macarons de Blanche
Blanche's Macaroons

MAKES ABOUT 2 DOZEN

1 cup granulated sugar

2 teaspoons grated orange peel

4½ ounces almond meal (see Note)

2 ounces all-purpose flour

2 eggs, at room temperature, separated, divided use

½ teaspoon salt

½ teaspoon vanilla

2 tablespoons unsalted butter, at room temperature

Sliced almonds, for garnish

Preheat the oven to 425 degrees F.

Line a large baking sheet with greased parchment paper. Set aside.

In a large bowl, combine the sugar and orange peel. Stir in the almond meal and the all-purpose flour. Set aside.

In a medium bowl, beat the 2 egg whites, salt, and vanilla until frothy. Combine with the flour/almond-meal mixture and 1 egg yolk. Save the second yolk for another use. Fold the butter into the mixture.

Place walnut-size portions of dough 2 inches apart on the parchment paper. With your fingers, press two or three sliced almonds into each portion of the dough. Bake until lightly browned, 8 to 9 minutes. Cool the macaroons on a rack.

Note: The terms *almond flour* and *almond meal* are often used interchangeably, though they are not the same. Almond meal comes from whole almonds (with skins). It is not as fine as almond flour made from skinless blanched almonds.

Pain d'Épices
Spice Cake

MAKES 1 LOAF

2 teaspoons baking soda

2 teaspoons aniseed powder

2 teaspoons allspice

1 teaspoon cinnamon

1½ cups rye flour

¾ cup oat flour

4 tablespoons unsalted butter

⅓ cup whole milk

⅔ cup honey

½ cup dark brown sugar

1 egg, at room temperature, lightly beaten

Butter and jam, for serving

In a large bowl, combine the baking soda, aniseed powder, allspice, cinnamon, rye flour, and oat flour. Set aside.

In a small saucepan over low heat, warm the butter and the whole milk. Transfer to a medium bowl and incorporate the honey, brown sugar, and the spice/flour mixture. Add the lightly beaten egg and mix well. Cover the bowl with a clean towel and let the dough rest on the kitchen counter for 1 hour.

Preheat the oven to 325 degrees F.

Line a loaf pan with greased parchment paper. Fill the pan evenly with the dough and bake until a knife inserted in the center comes out clean, 50 to 55 minutes. Unmold and cool on a rack. Serve the *pain d'épices* with butter and jam on the side.

Sidebar: A toasted slice of *pain d'épices* awaited me when I arrived home from *école primaire* in Casablanca. *Un petit goûter* (a little afternoon snack) was my mother's way of keeping my growling stomach at bay in the hours before dinner. The recipe for the intensely flavored spice cake is more than five centuries old, created by the Cistercian monks of Marienthal (Germany) in 1453. Today, *Le Musée du Pain d'Epices*, in the nearby town of Gertwiller, commemorates the friars' culinary achievement.

Crêpes à la Crème de Marrons et Ganache
Crêpes with Chestnut Cream and Ganache

SERVES 8

1 cup whole milk

6½ oz vacuum-packed chestnuts, steamed and shelled (see Note)

3 tablespoons granulated sugar, divided use

2 tablespoons heavy cream

2 teaspoons vanilla, divided use

8 crêpes (see page 87)

2 organic free-range eggs, separated (see Note)

2 tablespoons Cointreau orange liqueur

1½ teaspoons powdered sugar

2 tablespoons warm water

3 ounces semi-sweet chocolate, broken up

2 ounces unsalted butter

1 cup whipping cream

For the chestnut cream: In a medium saucepan over low heat, simmer the milk, chestnuts, and 2 tablespoons of the granulated sugar for 20 minutes. Remove from the heat and, with the mixture still in the pan, puree with a potato ricer. The mixture should attain the consistency of frosting. If it is too liquid, return to the heat and simmer for a few more minutes. If it is too thick, stir in more milk, one tablespoon at a time, until it is easily spreadable. Remove from the heat. Using the back of a wooden spoon, press the mixture through a medium and then a fine-mesh sieve. Stir in the cream and 1 teaspoon of the vanilla. Set the chestnut puree aside at room temperature to cool. Meanwhile, prepare the crêpes. Set aside.

For the ganache: In a medium bowl, whisk together the two egg yolks, Cointreau, powdered sugar, and warm water. Reserve the egg whites for another use. Set aside. Bring water to a boil in a double boiler. Remove from the heat and add the chocolate and the butter to the upper container. Stir until smooth. Into the egg yolk/Cointreau mixture, while stirring continuously, drizzle the molten chocolate/butter mixture. Set the ganache aside until serving.

⚜

In a chilled bowl, beat 1 cup of whipping cream, 1 tablespoon of granulated sugar, and remaining vanilla until stiff peaks form. Set aside until serving.

To serve, thinly spread each crêpe with chestnut cream, ganache, and whipped cream—or any combination thereof. Roll them up and garnish with a dollop of whipped cream.

Note: Chestnut trees bear fruit each year between September and October. In season, you can harvest recently fallen chestnuts or purchase them from specialty grocery stores or farmers' markets. Separate the nuts from their spiny burrs and freeze or store in an airtight container in the refrigerator. Before using, soak the chestnuts in water for several hours to soften their shells. With a sharp paring knife or serrated knife, score the rounded surface of the shells. In a medium saucepan, boil the chestnuts for 5 minutes and, with a slotted spoon, transfer them to a kitchen towel. Transfer them again to a preheated cast-iron skillet for 30 seconds in order to further expand the slits in the chestnuts' shells. Pour the nuts into another container and, when they are no longer too hot to handle, peel away their shells and their seed coats.

When using raw eggs, make sure they come from an organic, free-range source. Pregnant women and those who are immunosuppressed should avoid eating raw eggs. To pasteurize eggs, hold them for 3 to 5 minutes in water heated to 140–145 degrees F.

Crème Anglaise
Vanilla Custard

MAKES 2½ CUPS

⅓ cup granulated sugar
3 tablespoons cornstarch
⅛ teaspoon salt
2½ cups whole milk

2 eggs, at room temperature,
  separated, divided use
2 teaspoons vanilla extract

In a medium saucepan over medium heat, combine the sugar, cornstarch, salt, and milk. Whisk continuously until the mixture is warm to the touch. Remove from the heat. Transfer ¼ cup to a medium bowl and whisk in the 2 egg yolks. Reserve the whites for another use. Transfer this egg mixture back to the sugar/cornstarch/milk mixture in the saucepan. Return the saucepan to medium heat and whisk continuously until bubbles form and the custard coats the back of a spoon, 10 to 12 minutes. Do **not** boil. Remove the custard from the heat and stir in the vanilla. Strain through a fine-mesh sieve into a medium bowl to eliminate lumps. Cover the *crème anglaise* with plastic wrap to prevent a skin from forming. Serve at room temperature.

Flan à la Crème de Riz
Cream of Rice Flan

SERVES 6

Caramel:
1 cup granulated sugar
¼ teaspoon lemon juice
¼ cup water

Crème de Riz:
2⅔ cups whole milk
½ teaspoon salt
**¼ cup plus 1 tablespoon
    cream of rice cereal, uncooked**
**2 eggs, at room temperature,
    lightly beaten**
⅓ cup granulated sugar
2 teaspoons vanilla

Preheat the oven to 300 degrees F to warm an 8-inch x 12-inch baking dish containing six 3-inch, heat-proof ramekins.

Caramel: In a heavy-bottom saucepan over medium-high heat, bring the granulated sugar, lemon juice, and water to a boil. Lightly swirl the mixture but do **not** stir. Monitor the cooking process carefully. When the molten sugar turns amber (or reaches 300 degrees F on a candy thermometer), remove from the heat. Transfer the baking pan (with the ramekins) from the oven to the stovetop and pour equal amounts of molten caramel into each one. Swirl to coat the bottom of the ramekins and set aside.

Crème de Riz: Increase the oven temperature to 350 degrees F to bake the flan. In a medium saucepan, bring the milk and salt to a simmer. Stir, while gradually adding the cream of rice. Continue to stir until the mixture thickens somewhat. Remove the saucepan from the heat and slowly stir in the beaten eggs, sugar, and vanilla. Pour equal amounts of this mixture into the ramekins and add boiling water to the baking pan—until the water reaches half way up the sides of the ramekins. Return the baking pan to the oven and bake for 45 minutes.

Remove the baking pan from the oven and set the ramekins aside to cool for two hours. To unmold each ramekin, run a thin knife blade around the inside perimeter, cover with the concave side of a dessert plate, invert, and tap the bottom of the ramekin several times. Serve at room temperature.

Crème Pâtissière
Pastry Cream

Makes 5 cups

8 eggs, at room temperature
1 cup granulated sugar
1 cup all-purpose flour plus
     2 tablespoons

4 cups whole milk
4 teaspoons vanilla

Separate the eggs. Reserve the whites for another use. In a medium bowl, whisk the egg yolks and the granulated sugar until smooth. Add the flour and whisk until smooth.

In a medium saucepan over medium heat, bring the milk and the vanilla to a simmer but do **not** boil. Remove from the heat and, when the mixture has cooled somewhat, whisk a half cup into the bowl containing the egg yolk/sugar/flour mixture. While stirring, slowly add this tempered mixture to the milk and vanilla in the saucepan. Return the pan to the stove and, over low heat, continue to stir for a minute or two, until the pastry cream thickens. If lumps form, use a spatula to press the *Crème Pâtissière* through a sieve into a clean bowl. Cover the surface with plastic wrap, to prevent a skin from forming, and set aside. Refrigerate until ready to use.

Note: Crème pâtissière will last up to three days in a covered container in the refrigerator.

Sidebar: Crème pâtissière is often used as a base for fruit tarts.

Croissants aux Amandes
Almond Crescents

MAKES ABOUT 16

1 cup all-purpose flour
½ cup almond meal
   (see page 125)
½ cup granulated sugar

1 teaspoon baking powder
½ cup unsalted butter,
   chilled and cubed
1 cup powdered sugar

Preheat the oven to 325 degrees F.

Line a small baking sheet with greased parchment paper. Set aside.

In a large bowl, combine the flour, almond meal, granulated sugar, and baking powder. Add the butter and work the ingredients together using your fingers until the mixture resembles coarse bread crumbs. Gather up the dough with your hands and work it into a ball. On a floured work surface, cut this into 16 equal pieces and shape them into crescents. Using your fingers, pinch the tops to form a ridge and set, 2 inches apart, on the baking sheet.

Bake on the middle rack of the oven until firm, 25 to 30 minutes. Do **not** let the crescents turn brown. Remove the *croissants* from the oven and dust with powdered sugar. Store in a metal tin.

Pets-de-Nonne
Choux Pastry Puffs

MAKES 20 TO 24 PUFFS

6 ounces all-purpose flour
¼ teaspoon salt
1 tablespoon granulated sugar
2½ ounces unsalted butter
½ cup water
½ cup whole milk

3 eggs, at room temperature
3 cups vegetable oil, for frying
Apricot jam, for serving
  (see page 176)
Powdered sugar, for dusting

In a medium bowl combine the flour, salt, and granulated sugar. Set aside. In a heavy bottom saucepan, bring the butter, water, and milk to a boil. With a wooden spoon, stir in the flour/salt/sugar mixture and remove from the heat. Mix until the dough separates from the sides of the pan. Add the eggs, one at a time, and mix vigorously until each one is fully incorporated into the dough.

In a deep pan or a deep-fat fryer, bring 3 cups of vegetable oil to a low boil. One by one, drop walnut-size balls of dough into the simmering oil and cook until golden-brown puffs float to the surface, 8 to 10 minutes.

Using a slotted spoon, transfer the puffs onto paper towels to drain. Dust the *pets-de-nonne* with powdered sugar and serve warm, with apricot jam on the side.

Note: Literally, *Pets-de-Nonne* means "Nun's Farts." I have often wondered why no one thought to change the inelegant appellation. Not easily done, when, according to one food historian, the recipe traces its roots to the French Abbey of Marmoutier in the 15th century!

Ile Flottante aux Amandes Caramélisées
Floating Island with Caramelized Almonds

SERVES 6

4 organic eggs
⅛ teaspoon salt
⅛ teaspoon cream of tartar
¼ cup powdered sugar
½ teaspoon vanilla

3½ ounces whole blanched almonds
½ cup granulated sugar
¼ cup water
⅛ teaspoon lemon juice
Crème anglaise (see page 131)

Meringues: Preheat oven to 300 degrees F.

Separate the eggs. Beat the whites, salt, cream of tartar, and powdered sugar until soft peaks form. Fold in the vanilla. Reserve the yolks for another use. Line an 8-inch x 12-inch baking pan with parchment paper. Place 6 dollops of the vanilla/egg-white mixture onto the parchment paper. Set this pan inside a large baking pan. Fill the latter with enough boiling water to reach half-way up the outside of the pan containing the beaten egg whites. Transfer the bain-marie to the oven and bake for 15 minutes, or until the peaks of the meringues turn a golden brown. Remove from the oven and set the meringues aside to cool.

Almonds: Increase the oven temperature to 325 degrees F. Place the almonds on a cookie sheet and bake until lightly toasted, 8 to 10 minutes. Turn off the oven and leave the door ajar.

Caramelized Almonds: Line a baking pan with parchment paper and set aside. In a saucepan over medium heat, bring the granulated sugar, water, and lemon juice to a boil. Lightly swirl the mixture but do **not** stir. Watch the cooking process carefully. When the mixture turns amber (or reaches 300 degrees F on a candy thermometer), remove from the heat, quickly stir in the almonds, and spread over the parchment lined baking pan, separating as many as possible before they become too sticky. Reserve 2 dozen of the caramelized almonds for garnish. Transfer the rest to a work surface, cover with parchment paper, and coarsely crush using a heavy-bottom roasting pan.

Place 1 tablespoon of crushed caramelized almonds in the center of each dessert plate, top with a meringue, and garnish with the reserved whole caramelized almonds. Pool crème anglaise around the meringues to create "islands." Serve at room temperature.

⚜

Pommes au Four
Baked Apples

SERVES 4

4 Gravenstein or other baking apples
½ cup apricot jam (see page 176)

3 tablespoons chopped walnuts, toasted

Preheat the oven to 375 degrees F.

Core the upper two thirds of each apple, leaving the base intact. Widen the aperture at the stem end to 2 inches in diameter to make filling easier. Perforate the apple skins in several places with the tines of a fork. Fill the cores with a mixture of apricot jam and chopped walnuts. Fit the apples snugly into a baking pan containing ½ cup of water. Bake until the flesh is soft, 40 to 45 minutes. Serve warm.

Sidebar: Gravenstein apples were first described by French botanists in 1797. Almost a century-and-a-half later, in the years leading up to World War II, Gravenstein saplings were exported to Sonoma County, California, only to have their fruit return to France, in cans of apple sauce destined for US troops fighting on the Western Front.

Gâteau de Carottes
Carrot Cake

Serves 8

4 eggs, separated, divided use
¾ cup granulated sugar
4 ounces unsalted butter,
   at room temperature
2 oranges
2 tablespoons Cointreau
   orange liqueur
2 cups coarsely grated carrots

1⅓ cups almond flour
   (see Note page 125)
2 teaspoons baking powder
1 cup almond meal
   (see Note page 125)
1 teaspoon cream of tartar
4 tablespoons powdered sugar,
   divided use
1 cup heavy cream
½ teaspoon vanilla

Preheat the oven to 350 degrees F.

Grease the sides of a 9-inch cake pan and line the bottom with parchment paper.

In a large bowl, beat the egg yolks, granulated sugar, and the butter until the mixture forms ribbons. Reserve the egg whites. Zest and juice the oranges and set the zest aside. Stir ½ cup of the orange juice, the Cointreau, and the grated carrots into the egg yolk/sugar mixture.

In a medium bowl, mix the almond flour, baking powder, and almond meal. In increments, fold this into the egg yolk/grated-carrot mixture and set the resultant batter aside.

Beat the egg whites with the cream of tartar and 3 tablespoons of the powdered sugar until stiff peaks form. Fold into the batter, transfer to the cake pan, and bake on the middle rack of the oven until firm to the touch, 50 to 55 minutes. Cool on a rack and unmold on a serving platter.

In a chilled bowl, whip the heavy cream with the powdered sugar and the vanilla until stiff peaks form. Top individual servings of the *gâteau de carottes* with dollops of whipped cream and garnish with the reserved orange zest.

Bredele
Shortbread Cookies

MAKES ABOUT 35

8 ounces unsalted butter,
   at room temperature
½ cup granulated sugar
2 tablespoons grated lemon zest

2 tablespoons kirsch cherry brandy
2 cups all-purpose flour
Powdered sugar, for dusting

In a large bowl, cream the butter and the granulated sugar. Stir in the lemon zest and the kirsch. Add the flour, in increments, and blend until you obtain a smooth, firm dough.

On a lightly floured pastry board, divide the dough into two equal parts and roll out each one until ¼ inch thick. Refrigerate until the dough is firm to the touch, at least 2 hours. Cut the dough with a cookie cutter of your choice and set the cut-outs 1 inch apart on a parchment lined baking sheet.

Preheat the oven to 325 degrees F.

Bake the cookies on the middle rack of the oven until their edges turn golden brown, 20 to 25 minutes. Do **not** let the edges burn. Transfer the baking sheet to a cooling rack. Sprinkle the cookies with powdered sugar. Refrigerate for up to 2 weeks in an airtight container.

Tartelettes au Fromage Blanc
Cheesecake Tartlets

MAKES 8 TARTLETS

2⅔ cups all-purpose flour, divided use

3 tablespoons powdered sugar

1 teaspoon salt

4 ounces unsalted butter, chilled and cut into pieces

¼ cup ice water

2 eggs, separated, divided use

16 ounces fromage blanc or quark cheese

¼ cup whole milk

⅔ cup crème fraîche

2 teaspoons vanilla

½ cup baker's or superfine sugar

In a large bowl, combine 2 cups of the flour, powdered sugar, and salt. Create a well in the center and add the cubes of butter. Work the ingredients together using your fingers until the mixture resembles coarse bread crumbs. Add ¼ cup ice water, one tablespoon at a time, and continue working until the mixture forms a stiff dough. Knead for 10 to 15 seconds before shaping it into a disk. Cover the dough with plastic wrap and refrigerate for at least one hour or overnight.

In a medium bowl, beat the egg whites until stiff peaks form. Set aside. In a larger bowl, combine the egg yolks, fromage blanc, whole milk, crème fraîche, and vanilla. Mix in the remaining ⅔ cup of flour and the baker's sugar. Into this mixture, gently fold the beaten egg whites. Set the resultant cheesecake filling aside.

Remove the disk of dough from the refrigerator. Slice it into 8 wedges of equal size and shape each one into a ball. On a lightly floured work surface, roll these into rounds 4½ inches in diameter. Transfer one round of dough to a 4-inch tartlet pan and mold it to the bottom and sides. With a paring knife, trim the dough that extends over the rim and prick the bottom of the dough with the tines of a fork. Continue in this manner with the remaining seven rounds. Set the tartlet pans aside.

Preheat the oven to 350 degrees F.

To bake, pour equal amounts of the filling into the tartlet pans. Spread evenly with a spatula. Set the tartlet pans on a baking sheet and bake until the filling puffs up and turns golden brown, 40 to 45 minutes. Transfer to a rack to cool. Unmold the tartlets and serve at room temperature or chilled.

⚜

Tarte aux Prunes
Plum Tart

SERVES 8

2 cups all-purpose flour
3 tablespoons powdered sugar
1 teaspoon salt
4 ounces unsalted butter,
   chilled and cubed
1 egg yolk

2 pounds plums
3 tablespoons rum
2 tablespoons almond meal
   (see page 125)
⅓ cup dark brown sugar
2 teaspoons vanilla

In a large bowl, combine the flour, two tablespoons of the powdered sugar, and salt. Create a well in the center and add the butter. Combine this mixture using your fingers until it resembles coarse bread crumbs. Add the egg yolk, ¼ cup ice water, one tablespoon at a time, and work the mixture into a dough. Knead for 10 to 15 seconds before shaping it into a disk. Cover in plastic wrap and refrigerate for at least one hour.

Cut the plums in half, remove the pits, and slice the fruit into wedges. In a large bowl, combine the rum and remaining powdered sugar. Add the plums, mix to coat, macerate for 15 minutes, and drain.

Preheat the oven to 375 degrees F. Grease the fluted sides and removable base of a 10-inch tart pan.

Transfer the chilled dough to a lightly floured work surface, roll into a 12-inch round, and transfer to the tart pan. Gently mold the dough to the bottom and sides of the pan and let it drape over the rim. Trim the excess with a paring knife. Prick the dough in the bottom of the pan with the tines of a fork and sprinkle with the almond meal. Tightly arrange wedges of macerated plums over the bottom of the pan in a pattern of your choosing.

In a small bowl, mix the brown sugar and the vanilla. Set aside.

Place the tart pan on the middle rack of the oven and bake until the crust turns light gold, 35 to 40 minutes. Remove from the oven and evenly distribute the vanilla/brown-sugar mixture over the plums. Return the tart to the oven and bake until the sugar is melted and lightly caramelized, another 10 to 15 minutes. Transfer the *tarte aux prunes* to a rack to cool. Serve warm or at room temperature.

Tarte aux Pommes · Apple Tart
SERVES 8

2 cups all-purpose flour

2 tablespoons powdered sugar

1 teaspoon salt

4 ounces unsalted butter, cubed

4 eggs, at room temperature,
    divided use

¼ cup ice water

8 Gravenstein or other baking apples

2 tablespoons honey

1 cup warm water

1 oz unsalted butter, at room temp.

½ cup heavy cream

⅔ cup plus 2 tablespoons
    granulated sugar

1 teaspoon vanilla

Powdered sugar, for dusting

In a large bowl, combine the flour, powdered sugar, and salt. Create a well in the center and add the cubes of butter. Work the ingredients together using your fingers until the mixture resembles coarse bread crumbs. Separate one egg. Reserve the egg white for another use. Add the yolk and ¼ cup ice water, one tablespoon at a time, to the flour mixture and continue to work it into a dough. Knead for 10 to 15 seconds before shaping into a disk. Cover in plastic wrap and refrigerate for at least one hour or overnight.

Core, peel, and cut the apples into ¼-inch wedges. In a medium bowl, dissolve the honey in the warm water and add the sliced apples to prevent discoloration. Set aside.

Grease the fluted sides and removable base of a 10-inch tart pan. On a lightly floured work surface, roll the refrigerated dough into a 10-inch round. Transfer the round to the tart pan and gently mold it to the bottom and sides. Trim the excess dough with a paring knife. Prick the dough on the bottom of the pan with the tines of a fork. Set aside.

Preheat the oven to 425 degrees F.

Completely fill the tart pan with sliced apples arranged in a configuration of your choosing. Whisk together the heavy cream, 3 remaining eggs, granulated sugar, and vanilla. Pour this mixture over the sliced apples, being careful to fill any large gaps between the slices. Bake until the apples are lightly scorched along the edges, 35 to 40 minutes. Dust the *tarte aux pommes* with powdered sugar. Serve warm or at room temperature.

Sidebar: The apple trees in my great-grandfather's orchard may have included Pomme Lorraine, Pomme Christkindel, and Gravenstein, all native to *Le Grand Est* in France. The latter is today the most popular apple cultivar grown in California's Sonoma County.

Pudding de Pain avec Crème Anglaise
Bread Pudding with Vanilla Custard

SERVES 8

½ cup black currants
¼ cup rum
4 tablespoons unsalted butter, melted
8 cups stale bread or brioche, cubed and loosely packed
4 cups whole milk

½ cup granulated sugar
4 eggs, at room temperature, lightly beaten
¼ teaspoon salt
½ teaspoon cinnamon
Crème anglaise (see page 131)

Preheat the oven to 350 degrees F.

Soak the currants in the rum for at least 1 hour. Set aside.

Using 1 tablespoon of the melted butter, grease the bottom and sides of a 9-inch x 12-inch baking pan. Spread the cubes of bread over the bottom. Set aside.

In a medium saucepan over low heat, heat the milk and the sugar until warm to the touch. Remove from the heat and whisk in the eggs, salt, and cinnamon. Stir in the soaked currants, the rum, and the remaining 3 tablespoons of melted butter. Pour this milk/egg mixture over the cubes of bread, mix gently, and let stand for 15 minutes.

Bake until a knife inserted in the center comes out clean, 1 to 1¼ hours. Let stand for 30 minutes before serving, with crème anglaise on the side.

Zimmetkuchen
Cinnamon Coffee Cake with Crème Fraîche

SERVES 6

2 cups all-purpose flour
2 teaspoons baking powder
⅛ teaspoon salt
8 ounces unsalted butter,
    at room temperature
⅔ cup plus 2 teaspoons
    granulated sugar, divided use

1 egg, at room temperature
½ cup whole milk
1 teaspoon cinnamon
8 teaspoons crème fraîche

Preheat the oven to 350 degrees F.

Put a round of greased parchment paper at the bottom of an 8-inch, straight-sided baking pan. Set aside.

In a large bowl, mix the flour, baking powder, and salt. Set aside.

In another bowl, beat together the butter, ⅔ cup of the granulated sugar, the egg, and the milk until smooth. To the same bowl, in increments, mix in the dry ingredients until you obtain a thick batter. Pour this batter into the pie pan and level with a spatula. Bake for 20 minutes.

Meanwhile, combine the remaining sugar with the cinnamon. Remove the cake from the oven and sprinkle with the sugar/cinnamon mixture. Using a wine cork, create eight deep, uniformly distributed depressions in the cake. Fill each one with a teaspoon of crème fraîche. Return the *zimmetkuchen* to the oven and bake for another 20 minutes. Unmold when cool.

Beignets de Carnaval
Doughnuts for Carnaval

MAKES ABOUT 36

½ cup whole milk
¾ ounce fresh baker's yeast
3½ cups all-purpose flour
⅓ cup granulated sugar
½ teaspoon salt
2 ounces unsalted butter,
    at room temperature

1 tablespoon rum
2 eggs, at room temperature
2 cups vegetable oil, for frying
Powdered sugar, for dusting
Marmalade, for serving

Warm the milk to 110 degrees F. Add the yeast and set aside for 10 minutes, until the mixture forms bubbles.

In a large bowl, combine the flour, granulated sugar, and salt. Make a well in the center and add the yeast mixture and the butter. Mix thoroughly with your hands. Blend in the rum and the eggs, one egg at a time. Knead the resultant dough until it separates from the sides of the bowl. Cover with a clean cloth and let rise in a warm place for 1 hour.

On a floured work surface, using your hands, flatten the dough until ¼ inch thick. Cut into rounds with a 2-inch cookie cutter.

In a heavy pan or deep-fat fryer, heat the oil to 360 degrees F.

Fry the rounds of dough until golden brown, 2½ to 3 minutes on each side, and transfer to a baking sheet lined with paper towels to drain. Dust the *beignets* with powdered sugar and serve with marmalade on the side.

Pudding de Riz aux Cerises et Crème au Kirsch
Rice Pudding with Cherries and Kirsch Cream

SERVES 4

12 cherries, pitted
2 tablespoons water
4 tablespoons plus 2 teaspoons
   granulated sugar, divided use
½ cup Arborio rice
2 cups whole milk
1 teaspoon vanilla

2 eggs, separated, divided use
   (see Note)
1 tablespoon kirsch cherry brandy
2 teaspoons white vinegar
⅓ cup heavy cream
Mint leaves, for garnish

Cut 4 cherries in half and reserve for garnish. Quarter the rest and, in a small saucepan over medium heat, simmer them with 1 teaspoon of granulated sugar for 3 to 4 minutes. Set aside.

In a medium saucepan filled with boiling water, cook the rice for 3 minutes and pour into a sieve to drain. In the same pan over medium heat, bring the milk and 2 tablespoons (plus 1 teaspoon) of the sugar to a simmer. Add the parboiled rice and continue to simmer, stirring occasionally, until the rice is tender but still creamy, 20 to 25 minutes. Remove from the heat and stir in the vanilla and the simmered cherries.

In a medium bowl, whip the egg whites and the vinegar until stiff peaks form. Set aside. In another bowl, do the same with the heavy cream and set aside. In a third bowl, beat the egg yolks with the remaining granulated sugar and the kirsch. Into this mixture, gently fold both the whipped eggs and whipped cream to complete the *kirsch cream*.

To assemble the pudding, spoon ⅓ cup of the rice/simmered-cherry mixture into each ramekin. Top with kirsch cream and garnish with cherry halves and leaves of fresh mint.

Note: When using raw eggs, make sure they come from an organic, free-range source. Pregnant women and immunosuppressed patients should refrain from eating raw eggs. To pasteurize eggs, hold them for 3 to 5 minutes in water heated to 140–145 degrees F.

Bûche de Noël
Yule Log

SERVES 10

16 organic, free-range eggs, at
    room temperature (see Note)
⅓ cup Cointreau orange liqueur
2 tablespoons powdered sugar
⅛ teaspoon salt
¼ teaspoon cinnamon
⅓ cup warm water
12 ounces dark chocolate,
    broken into pieces

8 ounces unsalted butter
1 cup granulated sugar
1 cup all-purpose flour,
    loosely packed
1 tablespoon baking powder,
    tightly packed
1 (7-ounce) tube almond paste
Red and green food coloring

Separate 8 eggs. In a medium bowl, whisk together the yolks, Cointreau, powdered sugar, salt, cinnamon, and warm water. Set aside and reserve the egg whites for another use.

Bring water to a boil in a double boiler. Remove from the heat and add the chocolate and the butter to the upper container. Stir until smooth.

Into the egg yolk/Cointreau mixture, while stirring continuously, drizzle the molten chocolate/butter mixture. Transfer to the refrigerator or freezer and stir every ten minutes until the mixture attains the consistency of frosting.

Preheat the oven to 425 degrees F.

Grease an 11-inch x 17-inch baking pan and line it with greased parchment paper folded to conform to the pan's corners. In a mixing bowl, combine the remaining 8 eggs, granulated sugar, flour, and baking powder. Using an electric mixer, mix at high speed for 5 minutes. Pour the batter into the baking pan and bake for 5 to 7 minutes, until the cake turns a light golden brown. Do **not** overbake.

Flip the pan over onto a clean work surface covered with a clean, damp kitchen towel. Carefully peel away the parchment paper and, with the long side facing you, roll up the cake and towel together. Set aside to cool.

Meanwhile, mix the red and green food coloring with almond paste to create "berries" and "leaves" respectively. Set aside.

⚜

When the cake has cooled, carefully unroll it. Using a small offset icing spatula, spread half the chocolate mixture over its surface and roll it into a "log." Transfer to a serving platter. Spread the remaining chocolate mixture over the log and create a bark-like texture using the tines of a fork. Just before serving, decorate the bûche with the almond paste berries and leaves. Leftover cake should be covered, refrigerated, and eaten within three days..

Note: When using raw eggs, make sure they come from an organic, free-range source. Pregnant women and those who are immunosuppressed should avoid eating raw eggs. To pasteurize eggs, hold them for 3 to 5 minutes in water heated to 140–145 degrees F.

Sidebar: This family recipe for bûche de Noël spans five generations. Over the years, we have prepared the cake, not only during the holiday season, but for birthdays, anniversaries, graduations, and every so often, for the launch of a new book.

Caramel

MAKES 1 BATCH

1 cup granulated sugar   **½ cup water**
¼ teaspoon lemon juice

In a clean, heavy-bottom saucepan over medium-high heat, bring the granulated sugar, ¼ teaspoon lemon juice, and ½ cup of water to a boil. Lightly swirl but do **not** stir. Watch the cooking process carefully. When the mixture turns light amber or reaches 300 degrees F on a candy thermometer [this may take up to 15 minutes], remove from the heat and transfer to a heat-proof bowl. If you're making a *croquembouche* for the first time, don't be surprised if you have to prepare two or three batches of caramel to complete the recipe. If the caramel becomes too viscous, microwave for 10 to 12 seconds.

Note: Working with molten sugar is risky business. Even a small amount splashed on the skin can lead to a nasty and painful burn. For that reason, it is best to keep young children out of the kitchen. Wear long-sleeve clothing and use heat-resistant gloves when working with caramel.

Croquembouche
French Wedding Cake

MAKES 65 TO 70

Choux (puffs):
1 cup all-purpose flour
¼ teaspoon baking powder
½ teaspoon salt
1 tablespoon granulated sugar
1 cup water
4 ounces unsalted butter, cut up
4 eggs, at room temperature

Crème pâtissière:
(see page 135)

Caramel:
(see page 165)

Choux: In a bowl, combine the flour, baking powder, salt, and granulated sugar. Set aside.

In a heavy bottom saucepan over medium heat, bring the water to a boil. Add the butter and stir until melted. Remove the pan from the heat and immediately add the dry ingredients. Using a wooden spoon, mix vigorously until the dough separates from the sides of the pan. Transfer to the bowl of a stand-up mixer and, using a paddle attachment, mix the dough on medium speed. When the dough is no longer too hot to touch, add the eggs, one at a time, until each is fully incorporated and the mixture attains the consistency of a thick batter.

Preheat the oven to 425 degrees F.

Line a 12-inch x 17-inch heavy baking sheet with parchment paper. Using a piping bag with a ¼-inch round tip, pipe circular mounds of dough (1 inch in diameter and ½ inch high) 2 inches apart on the sheet. With a wet finger gently flatten the peaks. Bake for 10 minutes. Reduce heat to 375 degrees F and bake for another 10 minutes, until the puffs are golden brown. Turn off the oven and leave the door slightly ajar for 30 minutes to allow the puffs to dry completely. Set aside to cool. The puffs can be used immediately, placed in an airtight tin for use within two to three days, or frozen for another use.

To fill the puffs: Using a ¼-inch wooden dowel, poke a hole in the bottom of each puff. Attach a medium-round tip to a piping bag filled with crème pâtissière and fill the puffs. Set them aside.

Using poster paper, create a cone 7½ inches in diameter and 14 inches high. Seal the seams with edible glue. Tightly wrap the cone with parchment paper and seal the seams. Set the cone in the center of a 9-inch platter and use more glue to seal the perimeter, where the cone and platter meet. Set aside to dry.

Line a tray with parchment paper and set aside.

Meanwhile, prepare the caramel. Using a pair of tweezers, grasp a puff (chou) by the lip of the ¼-inch opening on its base. Dip the top of the puff into the molten caramel and place it, caramel side down, on the parchment-lined tray. Continue in this manner with the rest of the puffs. You may have to prepare several batches of caramel to complete this process.

To assemble the *croquembouche,* begin by preparing more caramel. Dip the side of a puff into the molten caramel and quickly bond it to the platter, making sure the puff's ¼-inch opening touches the surface of the cone. Continue in this manner to create a ring of puffs around the base of the cone. Assemble a second ring of puffs on top of the first, bonding the molten caramel to the sides of the puffs in the first ring. Continue adding concentric rings of decreasing diameter, until the tower is crowned with a solitary puff.

To decorate and reinforce the *croquembouche,* generously drizzle the face with caramel that has had a chance to cool somewhat and become more viscous. To serve, use kitchen shears to separate the choux from the *croquembouche.*

Sidebar: A *croquembouche* or *pièce montée*, is a towering pastry consisting of choux filled with crème pâtissière and encased in a glistening, amber web of caramel. It is the traditional centerpiece at a French wedding banquet.

Nicole teaches her grand-daughter Clara how to make *croquembouche*
(circa 1992)

Brioche
Alsatian Brioche

SERVES 8 TO 10

½ cup golden raisins
½ cup rum
1 ounce fresh baker's yeast
1 cup whole milk (warmed to 110–120 degrees F), divided use
⅔ cup granulated sugar, divided use

4 ounces plus 2 tablespoons unsalted butter, at room temperature
4 cups all-purpose flour
½ teaspoon salt
2 eggs, at room temperature
¾ cup sliced almonds, divided use

The night before, plump the raisins in the rum.

The following day, drain the raisins. Set aside. In a small bowl, dissolve the baker's yeast in 2 tablespoons of the warm milk. Sprinkle with 1 teaspoon of the sugar, cover, and set aside in a warm place until bubbles form, 10 to 15 minutes.

Dissolve 4 ounces of the butter in the remaining warm milk. Set aside.

In a large mixing bowl, combine the flour, salt, and the remaining sugar. Make a well in the center. Using your fingers, incorporate the eggs, one at a time. In increments, blend in the melted butter/milk mixture and then the yeast mixture. Transfer to a lightly floured work surface and knead for 10 to 15 minutes, frequently rounding up the sticky mass using a plastic scraper, until the dough pulls away from the work surface and becomes smooth, silky, and elastic. At this time, fold in ¼ cup of the almonds and the raisins. Return the dough to the mixing bowl, cover with a clean towel, and move to a warm place until it doubles in size, 1 to 2 hours.

Meanwhile, generously grease a 10-inch bundt pan with the remaining butter. Pour the remaining sliced almonds into the pan, cover with a large plate, and shake vigorously until the almonds adhere to the butter on the bottom and sides of the pan. Set aside.

⚜

When the dough has doubled in size, shape it into a ball. Poke a hole in the center to ease it over the bundt pan's "chimney" on the way to the bottom. Cover with a clean towel and move to a warm place until the dough rises just above the bundt pan's rim, about 1 hour.

Preheat the oven to 375 degrees F. Bake until the brioche is golden brown, 25 to 30 minutes. Let stand for 15 minutes before unmolding.

Sidebar: A heavy ceramic platter from Morocco has served me well over the years, especially when I'm making bread. Kneeling on a carpet behind my shallow 21-inch *g'saa* allows me to lean into the rigorous task of kneading dough. A stand mixer fitted with a dough hook would be easier, but then, I wouldn't get the workout.

Tradition warrants that this brioche (referred to as *kougelhopf* in Alsace) be baked in an eponymous high-sided ceramic mold produced by artisan potters in the town of Soufflenheim, not far from Haguenau.

Biscuits aux Amandes
Almond Macaroon Cookies

MAKES ABOUT 24

7 ounces granulated sugar
2 teaspoons grated orange peel
2 eggs, separated, divided use
4½ ounces almond meal
  (see page 125)

⅓ cup all-purpose flour
2 ounces unsalted butter,
  at room temperature
⅓ cup sliced almonds, toasted

Preheat the oven to 425 degrees F.

Mix the sugar with the grated orange peel. Set aside.

In a medium bowl, beat the two egg whites with one of the egg yolks. Reserve the second yolk for another use. In increments, stir the sugar/orange-peel mixture into the beaten eggs. Set aside.

In a small bowl, combine the almond meal, flour, and butter. Fold this into the egg/sugar/orange-peel mixture to complete the macaroon dough.

Line a baking sheet with greased parchment paper. Place ½-tablespoon portions of dough on the parchment paper, 2 inches apart. Flatten them with a wet fork into rounds 1½ inches in diameter. Press two or three almond slices into each one. Bake for 6 to 8 minutes. Do **not** let the edges of the macaroons turn brown. Using a spatula, transfer the cookies to a rack to cool.

Chapter Five

Preserves and Beverages

Confiture d'Abricots
Quick Apricot Jam

Conserves de Cerises et Fraises
Cherry and Strawberry Preserves

Marmelade aux Quatre Agrumes
Four-Citrus Marmalade

Confiture de Prunes
Plum Jam

Eau-de-Vie de Cerise
Cherry Brandy

Thé à la Verveine et au Miel
Lemon Verbena Tea with Honey

Confiture d'Abricots
Quick Apricot Jam

MAKES ABOUT 2 CUPS

1½ pounds apricots, unpeeled
2¾ cups granulated sugar

2 tablespoons fresh lemon juice

Cut the apricots in half. Remove and discard all but two of the pits. Crack these open to harvest the bitter kernels that will enhance the aroma of the jam.

Quarter the fruit and transfer to a bowl. Add the granulated sugar, whole apricot kernels, and lemon juice. Cover and set aside at room temperature for 2 to 3 hours. Transfer the apricot/sugar mixture (including kernels) to a large enamel pan and cook over medium heat, stirring frequently, for 30 minutes. On a chilled saucer, spoon out a bit of jam and pull your finger through it. The jam should not run. If it does, continue to simmer the jam for another 30 minutes. Discard the bitter kernels. Sterilize the jars according to your favorite processing recipe (see **Note**).

Note: For detailed instructions on preserving jams, visit the **National Home Food Preservation** website or the USDA canning website: https://nifa.usda.gov/blog/usdas-complete-guide-home-canning. The jam will keep in the refrigerator for 3 to 4 weeks or in the freezer for up to 3 months.

Conserves de Cerises et Fraises
Cherry and Strawberry Preserves

Makes 3 cups

1 pound pitted cherries, cleaned and cut in half
1 pound granulated sugar

½ pound medium strawberries, cleaned and cut in half

Place the cherries and the sugar in a bowl. Cover and macerate overnight.

The next day, strain the cherry juice into a medium enamel saucepan. Set the macerated cherries aside.

Bring the juice to a simmer and cook down until you obtain a light syrup, or the temperature reaches about 220 degrees F on a candy thermometer. Skim off the foam.

Add the macerated cherries and the strawberries all at once. Stir to mix and simmer for 20 to 30 minutes or until a little syrup forms a soft ball when dropped into ice water. This conserve does not thicken to the consistency of jam but remains syrupy. Store in clean jars and refrigerate.

Eau-de-Vie de Cerise
Cherry Brandy

Makes 3 cups

**1 pound unblemished
  sour cherries with stems,
  rinsed and dried**
**¾ cup granulated sugar,
  divided use**

3 cups vodka
1 stick cinnamon

Trim the cherry stems to 1 inch in length. In a one-liter glass jar with a metal-clasp lid, layer one third of the cherries and ¼ cup of the granulated sugar. Add two more layers of cherries and two more layers of sugar. Add the vodka and cinnamon stick and seal the jar. Store in a cool dark place for six weeks. Do **not** open the jar during this period. Serve chilled, as a digestif.

Sidebar: In a letter to her cousin Jacques Cerf, my mother wrote, "I have such fond childhood memories of Rosières . . . of the wooden barrel where your father concocted his *gnole* [home-made eau-de-vie] from his overripe Mirabelle plums or his cherries. I will never forget that delicate aroma!" In the days when Nicole and her sister, Martine, spent their summers in Châlons, one of their chores was to harvest the fruit for their grandfather's brandy.

Thé à la Verveine au Miel
Lemon Verbena Tea with Honey

SERVES 1

4 large leaves of lemon verbena, fresh or dried

1 cup boiling water
Honey, to taste

Steep 4 lemon verbena leaves in one cup of boiling water. Sweeten to taste with honey.

Photo Album

Michel and Berthilde
Neymarck, Blanche's parents

Blanche with daughters
Suzanne and Anny

Studio photograph of
Blanche in her mid 30s

Suzanne and Anny Lévy-Neymarck bookend
three younger cousins in this studio portrait.

Prosper introduces his officers to an official
from the French government

Prosper's military documents

Suzanne Lévy-Neymarck
as a flapper

Cousins Jacques Cerf and
Nicole Darmon, circa 1928

ATTENTION

Carte exclusivement réservée à la correspondance familiale

Il est permis d'écrire ci-dessous une correspondance de caractère familial de sept lignes ; mais il est strictement interdit d'écrire entre les lignes ou de donner des nouvelles qui n'auraient pas ce caractère. Il est indispensable d'écrire très lisiblement pour faciliter le contrôle des autorités allemandes.

Toute carte irrégulière dans la forme ou dans le fond ne sera pas acheminée ; sa valeur d'achat ne sera pas remboursée.

Nazi-sanctioned postcard from Prosper to his daughter Suzanne
in Casablanca requesting dried fruit, canned foods, rice, pasta, etc.

191

ROYAL AIR FORCE
CASABLANCA

No 3 F. T. I. U.

Grand

Farewell Ball

By kind permission of the Commanding Officer
SQUADRON LEADER V. C. EWENS

FAREWELL CASABLANCA

It is with regret that we of the R.A.F. leave our good friends in Casablanca.

Those of us who came to Morocco first, remember all too vividly the wonderful reception we had from our American, French and civilian Allies, this kindness being sustained right up to this event.

We remember with gratitude the formation of the Union Jack Club and the never-tiring efforts of this unselfish institution to make us comfortable.

We remember the kindness shewn to us individually by resident families and we recall happy hours spent at various American functions or in recreation made possible by American generosity. For all these things we are indeed grateful and it is with one voice that we wish our friends God-speed and Good Luck in the long days of peace to come.

C.C.F. Chandler's invitation to the Royal Air Force's Grand Farewell Ball, August 3rd, 1945

Prosper delivered his granddaughter Nicole in the upstairs bedroom of his home in Châlons-sur-Marne, on July 13, 1923

Bibliography

Bopp, Marie-Joseph, *Ma Ville à l'Heure Nazie*, Colmar 1940-1945, La Nuée Bleue, édition établie par Nicolas Stoskopf et Marie-Claire Vitoux, Strasbourg 2004

Cerf, Jacques, private correspondence, Morse family archives

Crisler, Jane, unpublished interview with Nicole Chandler and Martine Darmon Meyer, PhD. Milwaukee, WI. 1983

Ecrouves Detention Camp, https://francearchives.fr/findingaid/

Harmel, Kristin, *The Winemaker's Wife*, Gallery Books, an imprint of Simon and Schuster, NY 2019

Hinzelin, Emile, *Légendes et Contes d'Alsace*, Librairie Fernand Nathan, Paris, 1933

Iturbe, Antonio, *The Librarian of Auschwitz*, based on the true story of Auschwitz prisoner Dita Kraus, translated from the Spanish by Lilit Zekulin Thwaites, Henry Holt and Co, NY 2012.

Kahn, Albert, *Les archives de la Planète*, Albert Kahn and Jean Brunhes, Hachette Réalités, 1. La France. Paris, undated

Kahn, Albert, *Les archives de la Planète,* Albert Kahn and Jean Brunhes, Hachette Réalités, 2. Le Monde. Paris, undated

Lévy-Neymarck, Prosper, correspondence and private journal, Morse family archives

Acknowledgments

Mes profonds remerciements to Margaux Chépy of the Châlons-en-Champagne Tourist Office and local historian Marie-Josèphe Journet for their *patience et bonne humeur* in fielding and promptly resolving my numerous queries regarding the Lévy-Neymarcks of Châlons-sur-Marne; to Bruno Malthet, *Président de l'Association Nouvelle Catalaunie*; to my mother's octogenarian cousin in Paris, Jacqueline Karsenty, food writer, magazine editor, and expert in the field of French gastronomy; to childhood friends now living in France, authors Liz LeDeun and Joëlle Fruttero; and to Leïla Martin, Strasbourg-based food blogger and cooking instructor.

Thank you to Blanche's great-great-grandchildren—my nieces and nephew Clara, Janie, and Leon—in British Columbia, enthusiastic volunteers in my recipe-testing department; as well as Ellen Russell in her Tucson, Arizona kitchen.

And last but not least, thank you to Beau Kimbrel, of Kimbrel Designs, for his extraordinary tenacity and patience; to Lorna Johnson Print's eponymous owner for her punctilious and unrelenting attention to detail; and to my in-house food photographer, my most stalwart and dogged supporter, my husband, Owen.

Index

⚜

Praise for Bitter Sweet

"Bitter Sweet is a fascinating and harrowing account of the lives and worlds that were lost and disrupted in one French family during the wars and political convulsions of the 20th century. A selection of family recipes add a delicious poignancy to this story and remind us that cooking is an act of emotional memory."

—**Alexander Lobrano**, author, *My Place at the Table:*
A Recipe for a Delicious Life in Paris

"Kitty Morse's *Bitter Sweet* encompasses a narrative worthy of the best novels: a daughter faces the onerous task of going through her deceased mother's belongings and finds treasure buried amidst all the boxes and the closets overflowing with papers, photographs, and memories. But this is real life. There's an old, battered, leather valise hidden under a crocheted blanket. In it she finds, not the coins of Blackbeard nor the jewels of some long-dead duchess, but something worth far more than a few gold doubloons or sparkling rubies. From the moment Kitty opens the valise and discovers her French great-grandfather's journal and her Alsatian great-grandmother's handwritten recipes, she knows what she must do. And bittersweet it is. The book relates the tragedy of one Jewish family during one of the darkest periods of human history. Kitty's contribution to Holocaust literature is especially poignant and valuable and her great-grandmother's recipes ensure that, if nothing else, the tastes of life and love survive, both on the palate and in the heart."

—**Cynthia Bertelsen**, author of the award-winning *Stoves & Suitcases:*
Searching for Home in the World's Kitchens and
"A Hastiness of Cooks": A Practical Handbook for Deciphering
the Mysteries of Historic Recipes and Cookbooks

"Kitty Morse's latest book is a rare and rich telling of a family's journey in World War II, comprised from three perspectives: Kitty's tale of her discovery of an old valise containing her great-grandfather's diary, written in occupied France in 1940 and the genealogical archival research it engendered; heartbreaking entries from Prosper Lévy's impeccably written perspective of the increasing horror of Nazi occupation of Europe; and culminating with Kitty's passion for exploring culinary arts: the comfort and hope served up with treasured family recipes handed down through generations of women. Part history, part memoir, part cookbook, *Bitter Sweet* is an important addition both to Holocaust literature and the healing that traditional foods can offer our souls."

—**Kathi Diamant**, author, *Heart of the Zoo* and *Kafka's Last Love: The Mystery of Dora Diamant*

"This multi-sensory exploration of Kitty Morse's family's history and recipes is full of surprises. I can just imagine how delighted the author must have been stumbling on this treasure trove of family documents. *Bitter Sweet* is truly a bitter sweet tale about how part of a family was saved from Nazi-occupied France and the delicious, rediscovered recipes that show how French, Alsatian, yet culturally Jewish her family once was. . . ."

—**Joan Nathan**, author, *Quiches, Kugels, and Couscous* and *My Search for Jewish Cooking in France*

"In *Bitter Sweet*, cookbook author Kitty Morse brings us a very personal family history, complete with the translated wartime journal of her great-grandfather, a retired *médecin-colonel* in the French army and recipient of the *Légion d'honneur* in World War I, who ultimately did not survive World War II and whose family was deported to Auschwitz-Birkenau in 1944. Dr. Prosper Lévy's words and Kitty's historical context bring to life a rediscovered notebook and 65 family recipes. A true taste of Occupied France, from Morse's family table to yours."

—**Kristin Harmel**, *New York Times* bestselling author